Victory
in
Jesus

Bill Subritzky

Sovereign World

Sovereign World Ltd
PO Box 777
Tonbridge
Kent TN11 0ZS
England

ISBN 1 85240 324 1

Typeset by CRB Associates, Reepham, Norfolk
Cover design by CCD, www.ccdgroup.co.uk
Printed in England by Clays Ltd, St Ives plc.

Dedication

To my dear wife Pat,
who has been such a faithful helpmate
over many years

Contents

Foreword

In the years since the Lord, in His grace and mercy, first called me to Himself, I have found that the study of the word of God has been the very foundation of my walk with Jesus Christ. I have found the words of this quotation about the Bible to be so true:

> "This is the word of God, it is supernatural in origin, eternal in duration, inexpressible in value, infinite in scope, regenerative in power, infallible in authority, universal in interest, personal in application, inspired in totality. Read it through, write it down, pray in it, work it out and then pass it on."

Since I was born again of the Spirit of God some thirty-two years ago, I have made it my daily practice to spend time meditating upon the word of God. As I have done so, I have grown in faith and this has given me the strength and confidence to preach as an evangelist in many countries.

I have also been privileged to see many great miracles of healing and deliverance. I have found the word of God to be absolutely true in every respect. Hebrews 6:1 sets out the foundational principles of the word of God, namely repentance from dead works, faith toward God, the doctrine of baptisms, the laying on of hands, resurrection of the dead, and eternal judgment.

I have sought to present each of these doctrines in a balanced manner. I believe that as we ponder these doctrines, that our faith in Jesus Christ will grow. This has been my experience.

It is my earnest prayer that as this book is read, God will do a mighty work in the heart and mind of each reader.

I pray that this book will be widely used to the glory of God and the extension of His kingdom.

Bill Subritzky

Chapter 1

Understanding Repentance

There are six doctrines referred to in Hebrews 6:

> "Therefore, leaving the discussion of the elementary principles of Christ, let us go on to perfection, not laying again the foundation of repentance from dead works and of faith toward God, of the doctrine of baptisms, of laying on of hands, of resurrection of the dead, and of eternal judgment." (Hebrews 6:1–2)

These are the doctrines of:

1. repentance from dead works
2. faith toward God
3. doctrine of baptisms
4. laying on of hands
5. resurrection of the dead
6. eternal judgment.

The purpose of this study is to look at each of these doctrines in turn.

Looking firstly at the doctrine of repentance from dead works, we find it is the key to our walk with the Lord Jesus Christ. It is the key to salvation. It is the key to understanding God. It is the key to being born again and to receiving the baptism with the Holy Spirit. It is the key to healing, deliverance and every other aspect of our relationship with the living Jesus, and accordingly with God Himself.

What does repentance mean?

It is to change one's mind, to make a decision not to sin again.

It means to turn right around. In the above scripture, it is clear it also involves repentance from dead works.

With the coming of Jesus Christ as the Lamb of sacrifice, the works of the law of Moses are no longer a means to obtain right standing before God. The law of Moses required that various religious works were carried out, including the offering of sacrifices and many other types of offerings.

These "dead works" no longer justify us before God. They are works which have the appearance of religion, but do not relate to true faith in Jesus Christ. It means we are doing works which we think will justify us before God but which are not in accordance with His will. As the scripture says:

> *"For if the blood of bulls and goats and the ashes of a heifer, sprinkling the unclean, sanctifies for the purifying of the flesh, how much more shall the blood of Christ, who through the eternal Spirit offered Himself without spot to God, cleanse your conscience from dead works to serve the living God?"*
>
> (Hebrews 9:13–14)

True repentance leads us, first of all, to place our total faith and belief in the Son of God, Jesus Christ. In doing so, we turn away from dead religion and everything that is not centered upon Jesus Christ Himself. In the course of doing so, we repent from sin.

True repentance is quite different from remorse. Remorse is a feeling of deep sorrow or regret for our sins, but it does not in itself mean that we, in fact, repent from those sins. It is important to understand the difference.

The first words which Jesus preached were, *"Repent, for the kingdom of heaven is at hand"* (Matthew 4:17). John the Baptist had preached exactly the same words before Him (Matthew 3:2). Jesus is telling us to turn around and face in the opposite direction, that is, to turn from sin toward Him.

Before we are born again, our attention is focused on the things of the world and we are like those people of whom Paul speaks in his second letter to the Corinthians:

> *"But even if our gospel is veiled, it is veiled to those who are perishing, whose minds the god of this age has blinded, who do not believe, lest the light of the gospel of the glory of Christ, who is the image of God, should shine on them."*
>
> (2 Corinthians 4:3–4)

Repentance begins with God

Jesus said in John's Gospel:

> *"No one can come to Me unless the Father who sent Me draws him; and I will raise him up at the last day."* (John 6:44)

God is the one who always makes the first move. He begins to draw us to Himself and as He calls upon us, it is our responsibility to respond. Failure to respond to the call of God upon our heart for true repentance leads to eternal death; obedience leads to eternal life.

Paul meets Jesus

When Paul met Jesus Christ on the Damascus Road and was commissioned to preach the gospel, Jesus said to him:

> *"I will deliver you from the Jewish people, as well as from the Gentiles, to whom I now send you, to open their eyes, in order to turn them from darkness to light, and from the power of Satan to God, that they may receive forgiveness of sins and an inheritance among those who are sanctified by faith in Me."*
> (Acts 26:17–18)

Paul's obedience

Paul was obedient and we see the effect of his obedience in the next two verses:

> *"Therefore, King Agrippa, I was not disobedient to the heavenly vision, but declared first to those in Damascus and in Jerusalem, and throughout all the region of Judea, and then to the Gentiles, that they should repent, turn to God, and do works befitting repentance."* (Acts 26:19–20)

Change of mind

When we move in true repentance, a complete change of mind occurs. When I was born again of the Holy Spirit, I made a decision to turn 180 degrees from darkness to light and from the power of Satan to the power of God. As a result, I was not bothered with the effects of my previous sins.

Many people come to the Lord, but only partially repent. They do not make that full turn. Instead they only turn partially from their sin, with the result that the old sin is always drawing them back. They feel the pull back to their previous sins.

There must be a complete turning around, a cutting of cords of the past and a decision to face Jesus Christ absolutely. I believe this is why we see many people who are not healed or set free, because they have not made that complete turn. Perhaps they are still harboring bitterness, anger, unforgiveness or other sin in their hearts.

Unless we make that complete turn to Jesus Christ, then the powers of darkness will have a grip upon us.

Failure to open the rooms of the heart

In Proverbs it says:

> *"The spirit of a man is the lamp of the LORD,*
> *Searching all the inner depths of his heart."*   (Proverbs 20:27)

The literal meaning of *"inner depths of his heart"* is "rooms of the belly." This implies that our heart has rooms. If we do not open every room of our heart to the Lord, then Satan still has some control within us. Sometimes we open some of the rooms of our heart to Jesus Christ but keep others firmly shut because we do not wish to confess some of our sins. We hold that unconfessed sin in our heart with the result that it gives rise to demonic activity within us. We wonder why we feel oppressed or compelled, tormented or driven. It is because we have not opened every room of our heart to God. It is not until we do so that we have in fact truly repented.

One of the major sins of which Christians are often guilty, is that of unforgiveness. Just as God has, through Jesus Christ, forgiven us of all of our sins, so He expects us to forgive others. Jesus said:

> *"For if you forgive men their trespasses, your heavenly Father will also forgive you. But if you do not forgive men their trespasses, neither will your Father forgive your trespasses."*
> (Matthew 6:14–15)

From this scripture, it is clear that if we do not forgive others, then God will not forgive us.

In the parable of the unforgiving servant who was forgiven a great sum of money by his master but refused to forgive someone who owed him money, Jesus taught that the master was angry and handed the servant over to the torturers until he was able to pay all he owed. The master represents God who has forgiven us, but if we fail to forgive others then God promises to torment us:

> "And his master was angry, and delivered him to the torturers until he should pay all that was due to him. So My heavenly Father also will do to you if each of you, from his heart, does not forgive his brother his trespasses." (Matthew 18:34–35)

That is why we find so many Christians are tormented and, despite much prayer, are never delivered from demonic powers because God has, in effect, handed them over to the demons. Until true forgiveness and repentance takes place, they will not be set free.

The outworking of this unforgiveness can include sickness in their lives as well as mental torment and physical death.

Godly sorrow

In his second letter to the Corinthian Church, Paul rejoiced that their sorrow led to true repentance. He points out the difference between godly sorrow which produces repentance that leads to salvation and which is not to be regretted, and the sorrow of the world which only produces spiritual death:

> "Now I rejoice, not that you were made sorry, but that your sorrow led to repentance. For you were made sorry in a godly manner, that you might suffer loss from us in nothing. For godly sorrow produces repentance leading to salvation, not to be regretted; but the sorrow of the world produces death." (2 Corinthians 7:9–10)

Result of repentance

Then he goes on to point out the result of true godly sorrow:

> "For observe this very thing, that you sorrowed in a godly manner: What diligence it produced in you, what clearing of yourselves, what indignation, what fear, what vehement desire, what zeal, what vindication! In all things you proved yourselves to be clear in this matter." (2 Corinthians 7:11)

This should be the result of true repentance in our lives.

Works befitting repentance

When Paul met Jesus on the Damascus Road, Jesus told him to do works befitting repentance (Acts 26:19–20). What does this mean?

First of all we must understand that our faith must always rest in Jesus Christ. Works must never replace that faith. However, having turned to Jesus Christ, then it is important to do works that show the fruits of repentance. For example, sometimes we say we have forgiven others but we never do anything about putting things right with those people. We need to do some positive act such as writing to them and confessing our unforgiveness to them and showing them love.

I recently counseled a lady who had been tormented because of bitterness toward her father. She vehemently declared that she had forgiven her father and yet she would not let him into her house! She therefore showed no fruits of repentance in her life and the demonic powers were still tormenting her.

Many people seek deliverance from demonic power caused by unforgiveness. They claim that they have forgiven but there are no fruits of repentance in their lives and until this happens they are never set free.

No true faith without repentance

Repentance and faith go together. There can never be true faith without true repentance, as Paul made clear:

> *"You know ... how I kept back nothing that was helpful, but proclaimed it to you, and taught you publicly and from house to house, testifying to Jews, and also to Greeks, repentance toward God and faith toward our Lord Jesus Christ."*

(Acts 20:18, 20–21)

Commandment of Jesus

After His resurrection, Jesus commanded His disciples to go to all nations to preach the gospel. Again, we find the emphasis on "repentance."

> *"Then He said to them, 'Thus it is written, and thus it was necessary for the Christ to suffer and to rise from the dead the*

*third day, and that repentance and remission of sins should be
preached in His name to all nations, beginning at Jerusalem.' "*
(Luke 24:46–47)

First of all there must be repentance and then remission of sins.

Remorse

Remorse is feeling sorry for what we have done. It is an emotion
rather than a decision. Whereas, in the case of repentance, we
make a decision to change direction, in the case of remorse, we
do not. We just feel sorry for what we have done. Therefore,
remorse is quite different from repentance and does not bring
the same fruits as repentance.

Result of remorse

We have the sad case of Esau, who sold his birthright to his
brother, Jacob, for bread and a lentil stew. The Scriptures set out
the result:

*"lest there be any fornicator or profane person like Esau, who for
one morsel of food sold his birthright. For you know that
afterward, when he wanted to inherit the blessing, he was
rejected, for he found no place for repentance, though he sought
it diligently with tears."* (Hebrews 12:16–17)

Judas, who betrayed Jesus Christ, was remorseful when he saw
that Jesus had been condemned to death. However, his remorse
was not enough. He was not truly repentant. The result was that
he threw down the pieces of silver which had been the price for
his betrayal of Jesus, and went away and hanged himself.

Yes, worldly sorrow only leads to death. True godly repentance leads to life.

Result of failure to repent

The Scriptures contain clear warnings concerning the failure to
repent:

*"Do not be deceived, God is not mocked; for whatever a man
sows, that he will also reap. For he who sows to his flesh will of
the flesh reap corruption, but he who sows to the Spirit will of the
Spirit reap everlasting life."* (Galatians 6:7–8)

If we keep sowing fleshly things, that is following our own fleshly desires and ignoring God's will in our lives, then we are sowing corruption and we will have a corrupt reward. Those, however, who elect to follow Jesus Christ and obey His word, walk in the power of the Holy Spirit and accordingly will reap everlasting life. Jesus said:

> *"I say to you that likewise there will be more joy in heaven over one sinner who repents than over ninety-nine just persons who need no repentance."*   (Luke 15:7)

Prodigal son

A perfect example of repentance is given by Jesus in the parable of the prodigal son in Luke 15:11ff.

We find that this young man had gone away and wasted his inheritance. This is a picture of us before we are born again. We waste our eternal inheritance. On the cross, Jesus Christ has offered to us all the gift of eternal life, but if we waste that gift by turning away from Him and following the ways of the world, we are wasting our eternal inheritance.

This young man wasted his possessions with prodigal living and when a severe famine occurred in the land he began to find himself in difficulties. He went and *"joined himself to a citizen"* of the country to which he had gone.

Having been sent out to feed the pigs, he was so hungry he would have gladly filled his own stomach with the pods that the pigs ate, but nobody gave him anything.

Scripture then tells us that he came to himself. He realized that his own father's hired servants had enough to eat while he was dying of hunger. He then decided that he would go back home to his father. He would tell his father:

> *"Father, I have sinned against heaven and before you, and I am no longer worthy to be called your son. Make me like one of your hired servants."*   (Luke 15:18–19)

Many people think about doing something but never do anything about it. Some of us think that one day we will give our lives to Jesus, but in the meantime we follow our own desires. We forget that the day of the Lord comes like a thief in the night and that we should always be prepared to face our Maker.

We therefore do nothing about our salvation.

An alcoholic will do nothing about being set free from alcoholism until that person recognizes there is a problem. Similarly, a homosexual will not seek deliverance until he realizes he has a problem.

We must recognize we have a problem. Our problem is disobedience toward God. When we recognize we have that problem and truly turn back to Him, then we come into our inheritance, that is, eternal life.

This young man did something about it. He repented. His repentance is clear from verse 20 where we see him returning home to his father:

> *"But when he was still a great way off, his father saw him and had compassion, and ran and fell on his neck and kissed him."*
> (Luke 15:20)

It is interesting to see that, when his father saw him, he had compassion.

This represents us coming back to God. When we truly repent, God does not upbraid us or chastise us, He is full of compassion toward us and forgives us.

The father said to his servants:

> *" 'Bring out the best robe and put it on him, and put a ring on his hand and sandals on his feet. And bring the fatted calf here and kill it, and let us eat and be merry; for this my son was dead and is alive again; he was lost and is found.' And they began to be merry."*
> (Luke 15:22–24)

Robe of righteousness

The *"best robe"* represents the robe of righteousness which God puts on us as we come to Jesus Christ. He no longer sees our sin.

Ring

The ring represents our marriage to Jesus Christ. We join the body of Christ. We become part of the Bride and Jesus is the Bridegroom.

Sandals

The sandals on our feet represent the preparation of the gospel of peace. We walk with our feet shod with this gospel: that is the good news that Jesus Christ has come and has died to pay the penalty for our sins, that He has risen from the dead and is seated at the right hand of God.

Commission by Jesus Christ to His disciples after His death and resurrection

The first thing which Jesus Christ commissioned His disciples to do after His resurrection was to go out and preach the gospel:

> *"Then He said to them, 'Thus it is written, and thus it was necessary for the Christ to suffer and to rise from the dead the third day, and that repentance and remission of sins should be preached in His name to all nations, beginning at Jerusalem.'"*
>
> (Luke 24:46–47)

Summary

1. Among the first words which Jesus preached were, *"Repent, for the kingdom of God is at hand."*

2. There is a difference between remorse and repentance.

3. Remorse is being sorry for our sins; repentance is making a decision to turn right around from them, from darkness to light, from the power of Satan to the power of God.

4. Godly sorrow produces repentance that leads to salvation. This is true repentance, e.g. Paul the Apostle.

5. The sorrow of the world is only remorse and it produces death (Esau and Judas).

6. Godly repentance produces the fruit of godly fear in our lives, a vehement desire to follow God, a zeal for God and a knowledge that we are vindicated by God.

7. We need to do works befitting repentance.

Chapter 2

Understanding True Faith

True faith

The secret to obtaining true faith toward God is true repentance. Without true repentance, there can never be true faith. That is why repentance is the key to our walk with God.

Faith toward God is a gift from God. As we repent, this gift of God comes into our lives:

> *"For by grace you have been saved through faith, and that not of yourselves; it is the gift of God ... "* (Ephesians 2:8)

Faith defined

Faith is very clearly defined in the scripture:

> *"Now faith is the substance of things hoped for, the evidence of things not seen. For by it the elders obtained a good testimony. By faith we understand that the worlds were framed by the word of God, so that the things which are seen were not made of things which are visible."* (Hebrews 11:1–3)

Faith is believing something before we see it. The faith which God grants us has the quality of enabling us to believe things which we cannot see. Our walk of faith is not with our natural senses, but with the spiritual sense that God grants us:

> *"For we walk by faith, not by sight."* (2 Corinthians 5:7)

Examples of faith

Hebrews 11 sets out many examples of people whose lives were marked out by faith. Here are some of them:

1. Abraham

"By faith Abraham obeyed when he was called to go out to the place which he would receive as an inheritance. And he went out, not knowing where he was going. By faith he dwelt in the land of promise as in a foreign country, dwelling in tents with Isaac and Jacob, the heirs with him of the same promise; for he waited for the city which has foundations, whose builder and maker is God."   (Hebrews 11:8–10)

2. Sarah

"By faith Sarah herself also received strength to conceive seed, and she bore a child when she was past the age, because she judged Him faithful who had promised."   (Hebrews 11:11)

3. Isaac

"By faith Isaac blessed Jacob and Esau concerning things to come."   (Hebrews 11:20)

4. Jacob

"By faith Jacob, when he was dying, blessed each of the sons of Joseph, and worshiped, leaning on the top of his staff."
                                                        (Hebrews 11:21)

5. Joseph

"By faith Joseph, when he was dying, made mention of the departure of the children of Israel, and gave instructions concerning his bones."   (Hebrews 11:22)

6. Moses

"By faith Moses, when he became of age, refused to be called the son of Pharaoh's daughter, choosing rather to suffer affliction with the people of God than to enjoy the passing pleasures of sin, esteeming the reproach of Christ greater riches than the treasures in Egypt; for he looked to the reward. By faith he forsook Egypt,

not fearing the wrath of the king; for he endured as seeing Him who is invisible."   (Hebrews 11:24–27)

Without faith it is impossible to please God

"But without faith it is impossible to please Him, for he who comes to God must believe that He is, and that He is a rewarder of those who diligently seek Him."   (Hebrews 11:6)

The author and finisher of our faith

Jesus Christ is the author and finisher of our faith:

"looking unto Jesus, the author and finisher of our faith, who for the joy that was set before Him endured the cross, despising the shame, and has sat down at the right hand of the throne of God."   (Hebrews 12:2)

Having faith in God

Jesus told us to have faith in God:

"For assuredly, I say to you, whoever says to this mountain, 'Be removed and be cast into the sea,' and does not doubt in his heart, but believes that those things he says will come to pass, he will have whatever he says. Therefore I say to you, whatever things you ask when you pray, believe that you receive them, and you will have them."   (Mark 11:23–24)

This is perhaps one of the most widely quoted scriptures concerning faith itself. Many times it has been taken completely out of context and without regard to the remainder of the word of God. One of the scriptures which should be placed alongside it is the following:

"Now this is the confidence that we have in Him, that if we ask anything according to His will, He hears us. And if we know that He hears us, whatever we ask, we know that we have the petitions that we have asked of Him."   (1 John 5:14–15)

Obviously then when we pray in faith, we should pray in accordance with the will of God. God's will is made clear to us as we read His whole word.

Faith as a gift

It is by God's favor that we are saved, it is not by our own works.
God grants us this faith as a gift from Himself, to bring us to
salvation. Jesus made this very clear:

> *"Therefore I have said to you that no one can come to Me unless
> it has been granted to him by My Father."*   (John 6:65)

God draws us to Himself

Nobody comes under the sound of the gospel of Jesus Christ or
reads about Him by chance. It is in the design of God. It is part
of God's plan to call us to Him.

Whenever I conduct an evangelistic meeting, I tell the people
that they are not there by chance. It has been God's plan to
bring them to that meeting to listen to the gospel being
preached.

The gospel of Jesus Christ is set out in 1 Corinthians:

> *"For I delivered to you first of all that which I also received: that
> Christ died for our sins according to the Scriptures, and that He
> was buried, and that He rose again the third day according to the
> Scriptures . . ."*   (1 Corinthians 15:3–4)

Every opportunity should be taken of presenting the gospel,
that is the atoning death and resurrection of Jesus Christ. As we
listen to that gospel, the Holy Spirit speaks to us. Jesus has died
for each one of us and paid the penalty for our sins; as we turn
to Him He gives us the gift of eternal life. The Holy Spirit is
drawing us toward God. It is at that point, as we listen to the tug
of the Holy Spirit in our hearts, that we can make a decision for
the Lord. God does His part. He draws us to Him.

I always remember that I felt that sense of being drawn
toward God for some years before I finally made a decision.
Although I had been going to church for many years, I did not
know Jesus Christ as my personal Savior. In two Billy Graham
meetings I refused to go forward. My pride held me back. It was
only as the situation in my life and marriage worsened that I
was prepared to listen to the call of God in my heart.

However, God still required me to do something about it, and
that was to make a decision for Him. God leaves that decision to
us. One night in a meeting I felt that I could no longer delay.

The pull of God on my heart was so strong and yet my fleshly desires were rebelling. Nevertheless, as the meeting progressed and as the preacher asked everybody to bow their heads and close their eyes, I felt the call of God becoming stronger by the moment.

Finally, when I could resist no more and I knew God was speaking to me, I looked around to confirm that the people were obeying the preacher, and that every head was bowed and every eye was shut! When I was sure this was so, then I put my hand up and down in a moment of time. However, God saw my hand.

Subsequently, I completed an essential requirement of surrender to God, namely confessing Him, Jesus Christ, as my Lord and Savior before others.

The word is near us, even in our mouth and our heart:

> *"But what does it say? 'The word is near you, in your mouth and in your heart' (that is, the word of faith which we preach): that if you confess with your mouth the Lord Jesus and believe in your heart that God has raised Him from the dead, you will be saved. For with the heart one believes unto righteousness, and with the mouth confession is made unto salvation."*
>
> (Romans 10:8–10)

True belief

It is with our heart that we believe and so come to full right standing before God. It is with our mouth that we make our confession.

Jesus Christ has told us that if we confess His name before men, He will confess our name before God and the angels. If we deny Him before men, He will deny us before God and the angels:

> *"Therefore whoever confesses Me before men, him I will also confess before My Father who is in heaven. But whoever denies Me before men, him I will also deny before My Father who is in heaven."* (Matthew 10:32–33)

The wind of the Holy Spirit

Jesus explained how the Holy Spirit moves by referring to the wind:

> *"The wind blows where it wishes, and you hear the sound of it,*
> *but cannot tell where it comes from and where it goes. So is*
> *everyone who is born of the Spirit."*   (John 3:8)

The Holy Spirit moves across the earth, blowing, so to speak, as God wills. When the Holy Spirit comes upon us and draws us to God, that is the time when we need to respond with all of our heart.

Sitting in church is not enough. We need to be born again of the Spirit of God. I sat in church for twenty years without knowing Jesus Christ as my personal Savior. Attending church does not of itself save us any more than being born in a stable makes us a horse. Belonging to a church does not save us. No church is the way to God.

Jesus Christ is the only way, the only truth and the only life. The church should point us to Jesus Christ, but we need to have that personal experience with Him.

Being baptized in water is not enough. We need to be born again of the Spirit of God, that is, we need to make a decision to follow Jesus Christ and to respond to the calling of the Holy Spirit upon our lives. As Jesus said:

> *"Most assuredly, I say to you, unless one is born of water and the*
> *Spirit, he cannot enter the kingdom of God. That which is born*
> *of the flesh is flesh, and that which is born of the Spirit is spirit.*
> *Do not marvel that I said to you, 'You must be born again.'"*
>   (John 3:5–7)

Turning from the world

Thus, we must place our entire faith in God. The things of the world should no longer draw us. As the first letter of John says:

> *"Do not love the world or the things in the world. If anyone loves*
> *the world, the love of the Father is not in him. For all that is in*
> *the world – the lust of the flesh, the lust of the eyes, and the pride*
> *of life – is not of the Father but is of the world. And the world is*
> *passing away, and the lust of it; but he who does the will of God*
> *abides forever."*   (1 John 2:15–17)

As we grow in faith toward God, then we can believe the 7,000 or more promises in His Word. However, we will never have that faith without continuing in true repentance toward God.

If we continue to walk in the faith that God gives us, reading His Word daily, praying daily and fellowshipping with believers who really love and trust the Lord, then our faith toward God grows. This faith is not stagnant, it is living.

When I was born again of the Spirit of God, He placed a flame in my heart, which has never gone out. It is the flame of the Holy Spirit.

My wife, Pat, and our children had the same experience. This is the reason why, as the years go by, we never cease to proclaim publicly at every opportunity the good news about Jesus Christ.

Have you got that flame in your heart? If you are not on fire for God, then perhaps you need to go back and start again. Maybe you should re-examine your life to ensure that you have truly repented from every aspect of sin and that you have truly turned in full repentance toward God, so that His faith can flow into you as a mighty power.

A sure sign of being born again of the Spirit of God is an insatiable thirst for the word of God.

Sometimes people still have some form of blockage in their walk with God, even though they do their best to break that bondage. It is in those cases that I suggest that they look at the question of inherited sin.

Sins of the fathers

God has said in the Ten Commandments:

> *"You shall not make for yourself any carved image, or any likeness of anything that is in heaven above, or that is in the earth beneath, or that is in the water under the earth; you shall not bow down to them nor serve them. For I, the LORD your God, am a jealous God, visiting the iniquity of the fathers on the children to the third and fourth generations of those who hate Me ... "* (Exodus 20:4–5)

We note that the iniquity of the fathers is visited on the children to the third and fourth generations of those who hate Him. Hating God really means that we do not follow Him. Those who hate Him are those who ignore Him or refuse to allow Him to become the center of their lives through Jesus Christ. It does not necessarily mean an act of hatred toward God, but rather sinning by not turning toward Him with all our heart.

Furthermore, that hatred can be exhibited by following false gods such as being involved in the occult. Many of our ancestors have done that, namely have gone to fortune tellers or witch doctors or they, themselves, have relied on lucky charms and similar occultic objects.

The effect of this has been to allow familiar spirits to enter the generations and follow down the family line. These familiar spirits seek to block us from the knowledge of God.

If, despite your best efforts at repentance, you still feel there is some blockage between you and God, then curses can be the cause of the problem. The scripture says:

> *" 'Cursed is the one who treats his father or his mother with contempt.' And all the people shall say, 'Amen!' "*
>
> (Deuteronomy 27:16)

Honoring of parents

> *" 'Honor your father and mother,' which is the first commandment with promise: that it may be well with you and you may live long on the earth."*   (Ephesians 6:2–3)

We need to honor our mother and father, no matter what they have done to us. It is only by the power of the Holy Spirit that we can do this, because many of us may have been badly treated by our mother or father or may not even know them. As we honor our parents and forgive them, we are able to renounce their sins and the sins of our ancestors and thus appropriate fully the blessing of God:

> *"Christ has redeemed us from the curse of the law, having become a curse for us (for it is written, 'Cursed is everyone who hangs on a tree'), that the blessing of Abraham might come upon the Gentiles in Christ Jesus, that we might receive the promise of the Spirit through faith."*   (Galatians 3:13–14)

When we honor our parents and renounce their sins and the sins of our ancestors, then these blockages will disappear.

A suitable prayer is suggested at the end of this section.

Summary

1. Faith toward God is a gift.

2. Faith toward God will come only as we truly repent.

3. We are saved through faith. Saving faith is a gift of God:

    "For by grace you have been saved through faith, and that not of yourselves; it is the gift of God ... "

    (Ephesians 2:8)

4. Jesus Christ is the author and the finisher of our faith.

5. We are exhorted to have faith in God.

6. No one can come to Jesus unless it is first granted to him by God.

    "And He said, 'Therefore I have said to you that no one can come to Me unless it has been granted to him by My Father.'" (John 6:65)

7. Like the wind, the Holy Spirit blows where He wishes, but when He comes to us, it is our time to turn to God and repent.

    "The wind blows where it wishes, and you hear the sound of it, but cannot tell where it comes from and where it goes. So is everyone who is born of the Spirit." (John 3:8)

8. We need to confess with our mouth the Lord Jesus and believe in our heart that God has raised Him from the dead and in that way we will be saved.

    "that if you confess with your mouth the Lord Jesus and believe in your heart that God has raised Him from the dead, you will be saved." (Romans 10:9)

9. As we do so, we are born again of the Spirit of God:

    "Most assuredly, I say to you, unless one is born of water and the Spirit, he cannot enter the kingdom of God."

    (John 3:5)

10. We should turn absolutely from the things of the world and place our entire faith in God.

11. We should honor our parents and renounce their sins.

Prayer

"Dear Heavenly Father, I come to You in the name of Jesus Christ.

I thank You, Lord, for Your love for me. I confess that Jesus Christ is my Lord and my Savior and that He died and rose again from the dead.

I believe that through the blood of Jesus Christ I have been redeemed from the hand of the devil.

I believe that through the blood of Jesus Christ all my sins have been forgiven.

I believe that through the blood of Jesus Christ I have been sanctified, made holy to God.

I believe that through the blood of Jesus Christ I have been justified just as if I had never sinned.

I now confess all my sins.

I confess that in my own strength I have been unable to defeat the attacks of the enemy.

I specifically renounce the following sexual sins ....

....

I confess I have been wrong.

I renounce all pleasure connected with these sins.

I now turn from my sin.

I ask You, Father, to forgive me all that is past and give me discernment when the temptation arises, and the strength to resist it.

I ask You to heal my memories and to heal the hurts and forgive me in Jesus' name.

I also specifically renounce any other sins such as rejection and unforgiveness.

I especially forgive the following persons ....

....

I specifically honor my parents and I forgive them.

I renounce my own sins and the sins of my ancestors in the name of Jesus Christ.

I especially renounce all idolatry, witchcraft and everything of the occult and all the hidden things of darkness.

I call upon You, Lord Jesus, to set me free from every demonic power that has affected me.

Lord, I now renounce Satan and all his works. I hate his demons. I count them my enemies in the name of Jesus.

I loose myself from every dark spirit, from every evil influence, from every satanic bondage, from any spirit in me that is not the Spirit of God. I command all such spirits to leave me now in the name of Jesus.

I call upon You, Lord Jesus, to set me free from every demonic power that has affected me.

In the name of Jesus Christ, Risen Savior, I command every demonic power that has lived within me or oppressed me to leave me now in the name of Jesus Christ.

I declare that I am a child of the Living God and that Satan has no right to inhabit any part of me or to oppress me. I thank You, Lord Jesus, and I give You the glory.

Amen."

Chapter 3

How We Receive Faith

The spiritual man versus the natural man

Immediately after I was born again, I began reading the Bible. I had previously tried over a number of years to read it, but it never made sense to me. I would read one verse, then a second, but by the time I read the third I had forgotten what the first had said.

That is why 1 Corinthians 2:14 says:

> *"But the natural man does not receive the things of the Spirit of God, for they are foolishness to him; nor can he know them, because they are spiritually discerned."*

Accordingly we are told:

> *"For what man knows the things of a man except the spirit of the man which is in him? Even so no one knows the things of God except the Spirit of God."* (1 Corinthians 2:11)

The Bible is a closed book to those who are not born again of the Spirit of God.

When I began to read the Bible, I did so on a systematic basis. I divided it into four parts, reading a portion each day so that over the course of a year, I have read the Old Testament each three months, the Gospels each fourteen days and Acts to Revelation every twenty-one days. This provides a continuous foundation for my walk with Jesus Christ.

As I did this, I still did not understand large portions of it. However, I took the view that it was the word of God and I simply believed it even though I didn't understand it.

By coming to the word of God as a little child throughout all of these years, and simply believing it, my understanding has grown and many of the so-called difficult portions have been made clear to me by the Spirit of God. I believe the following is a true statement:

> "This is the word of God, it is supernatural in origin, eternal in duration, inexpressible in value, infinite in scope, regenerative in power, infallible in authority, universal in interest, personal in application, inspired in totality. Read it through, write it down, pray it in, work it out, and then pass it on."

Belief of a little child

In approaching the word of God, we need to come to it as a little child. As Jesus said in Matthew 18:

> *"Assuredly, I say to you, unless you are converted and become as little children, you will by no means enter the kingdom of heaven."* (Matthew 18:3)

The word of God is settled forever

We must understand that the word of God is unchanging. It is settled forever:

> *"Forever, O LORD,*
> *Your word is settled in heaven."* (Psalm 119:89)

And it shall stand forever:

> *"The grass withers, the flower fades,*
> *But the word of our God stands forever."* (Isaiah 40:8)

Hearing and doing

It is one thing to hear the word of God, but it is another thing to do it. Jesus emphasized this difference as follows:

> *"Therefore whoever hears these sayings of Mine, and does them, I will liken him to a wise man who built his house on the rock: and the rain descended, the floods came, and the winds blew and beat on that house; and it did not fall, for it was founded on the rock. Now everyone who hears these sayings of Mine, and*

does not do them, will be like a foolish man who built his house
on the sand: and the rain descended, the floods came, and the
winds blew and beat on that house; and it fell. And great was its
fall."   (Matthew 7:24–27)

Here He is speaking of hearing and doing the word of God. We
are not only called upon to hear and to listen to the word of
God, both as we read it and as we hear others preaching it, but
also to carry out what it has to say. As we begin to act upon the
word of God, then our faith grows.

As a preacher and teacher, I have learnt that if I confess the
word of God by speaking it out, my own faith grows. For
example, if I give several days' teaching, I find at the end of
that time that, having spoken the word of God on many
occasions, my faith is at a greater depth than it was when I
began. The word of God does change us from the inside out.

The word of God is a lamp to our feet

"Your word is a lamp to my feet
And a light to my path."   (Psalm 119:105)

It gives light and understanding to us.

"The entrance of Your words gives light;
It gives understanding to the simple."   (Psalm 119:130)

It can be like a hammer

" 'Is not My word like a fire?' says the LORD,
'And like a hammer that breaks the rock in pieces?' "
                                                 (Jeremiah 23:29)

As we hear the word of God and act upon it, then sin can be
crushed out of our lives. Nothing can stand against the word of
God.

Many times when I am ministering in deliverance and casting
out demons, I quote the word of God to the demons. As they
recognize the authority with which I speak as a minister of Jesus
Christ and also recognize that I believe the words that I am
speaking, then they begin to tremble and scream. It is then that
they leave the person. When I speak out the word of God with
belief, I sense an authority coming through me which is of God.
Demons sense the same authority and then flee.

The word of God is pure

The words of God are pure: as the scripture says, they are purified seven times:

> *"The words of the LORD are pure words,*
> *Like silver tried in a furnace of earth,*
> *Purified seven times."* (Psalm 12:6)

Faith comes by hearing and hearing by the word of God

As we are prepared to listen to God, then our faith in Him grows. We can listen to the word of God by reading the Bible and hearing the word preached. While we are reading the Bible, God will speak to our inner spiritual ear. He will talk to our spirit and encourage our faith.

For this reason it is good to hear the gospel preached with power and with belief. As this happens, the power of God falls in a meeting and the anointing of God is present.

When a person is anointed to teach from the word, miracles of healing and deliverance can occur, even while the teaching is taking place. As the attention of the listeners is gripped by the word of God, the Spirit of God is able to move upon them and through them, increasing their faith to believe what they are hearing.

The scripture says:

> *"So then faith comes by hearing, and hearing by the word of God."* (Romans 10:17)

We should be careful to listen with an attentive ear when the word of God is being preached. As we do so, God is able to bless us. That is why Jesus said:

> *"Therefore take heed how you hear. For whoever has, to him more will be given; and whoever does not have, even what he seems to have will be taken from him."* (Luke 8:18)

The word of God builds us up

When Paul was giving his final message to the elders of Ephesus, he reminded them of the power of the word of God:

> *"So now, brethren, I commend you to God and to the word of His grace, which is able to build you up and give you an inheritance among all those who are sanctified."*   (Acts 20:32)

Jude also reminds us to build ourselves up:

> *"But you, beloved, building yourselves up on your most holy faith, praying in the Holy Spirit ... "*   (Jude 1:20)

As we read the word of God and pray in the Holy Spirit, remembering always the power of the blood of Jesus, then our faith grows mightily.

Testing of our faith

The Bible says that the testing of our faith produces patience. When we pray to God in faith, we should not doubt because those who doubt are like a wave of the sea, driven and tossed by the wind. Such people will receive nothing from the Lord:

> *" ... knowing that the testing of your faith produces patience. But let patience have its perfect work, that you may be perfect and complete, lacking nothing. If any of you lacks wisdom, let him ask of God, who gives to all liberally and without reproach, and it will be given to him. But let him ask in faith, with no doubting, for he who doubts is like a wave of the sea driven and tossed by the wind. For let not that man suppose that he will receive anything from the Lord; he is a double-minded man, unstable in all his ways."*   (James 1:3–8)

Summary

1. The natural mind does not understand the things of the Spirit of God because they are spiritually understood.

2. We should come to the word of God and believe it as a little child.

3. The word of God is unchangeable. It is forever settled in heaven.

4. We should not only listen to the word of God, but do it.

5. The word of God is a lamp to our feet.

6. It can be like a hammer that breaks rocks.

7. The word of God is pure.

8. As we listen to the word of God with a spiritual ear and as we read it, the Holy Spirit helps us and our faith is built up.

9. The testing of our faith produces patience.

10. When we ask in faith we should not doubt, otherwise we are like the double-minded man, unstable in all his ways.

Chapter 4

How God's Word Works in Us

As we believe God's word, it actually works in us. This is confirmed in Scripture.

Effective working of the word of God

> *"For this reason we also thank God without ceasing, because when you received the word of God which you heard from us, you welcomed it not as the word of men, but as it is in truth, the word of God, which also effectively works in you who believe."*
>
> (1 Thessalonians 2:13)

Guidance

The word of God provides guidance for us in all aspects of our life. We are told in Psalms:

> *"Your word is a lamp to my feet*
> *And a light to my path."* (Psalm 119:105)

Mercy and truth

The word of God tells us not to let mercy and truth leave us, but to bind them around our neck and to write them on the tablet of our heart. By doing so, we

> *" . . . find favor and high esteem*
> *In the sight of God and man."* (Proverbs 3:4)

Understanding

Again, the word of God tells us to trust the Lord with all our heart and not to lean on our own understanding:

> *"In all your ways acknowledge Him,*
> *And He shall direct your paths."*   (Proverbs 3:6)

Prosperity

We have the promise of prosperity from the word of God:

> *"Honor the L*ORD* with your possessions,*
> *And with the firstfruits of all your increase;*
> *So your barns will be filled with plenty,*
> *And your vats will overflow with new wine."*
>   (Proverbs 3:9–10)

Health

We are told that if we give attention to God's words, then it is health to our flesh:

> *"My son, give attention to my words;*
> *Incline your ear to my sayings.*
> *Do not let them depart from your eyes;*
> *Keep them in the midst of your heart;*
> *For they are life to those who find them,*
> *And health to all their flesh."*   (Proverbs 4:20–22)

> *"Do not be wise in your own eyes;*
> *Fear the L*ORD* and depart from evil.*
> *It will be health to your flesh,*
> *And strength to your bones."*   (Proverbs 3:7–8)

Deliverance

The word of God promises us deliverance in the day of trouble:

> *"Call upon Me in the day of trouble;*
> *I will deliver you, and you shall glorify Me."*   (Psalm 50:15)

One of the ways in which the word of God protects us and causes our faith to increase is by warning us against sin. If we deliberately sin, then a barrier develops between God and us:

"Behold, the LORD'*s hand is not shortened,*
That it cannot save;
Nor His ear heavy,
That it cannot hear.
But your iniquities have separated you from your God;
And your sins have hidden His face from you,
So that He will not hear."   (Isaiah 59:1–2)

Should be hidden in our heart

However, David suggests a remedy against the possibility of sin in our lives:

"Your word I have hidden in my heart,
That I might not sin against You."   (Psalm 119:11)

The word of God gives protection

As we allow the word of God to be stored up within us and hidden in our heart, then it is always available to us in times of emergency and temptation:

"Concerning the works of men,
By the word of Your lips,
I have kept away from the paths of the destroyer."
                                                (Psalm 17:4)

The word of God gives wisdom and discernment

If we allow the word of God into our heart and mind, reading it daily and acting upon it, then God is able to direct our paths away from sin.

When we treasure God's words within us and allow our inner ear of understanding to hear them and believe them, then God gives us discernment and knowledge as well as wisdom:

"My son, if you receive my words,
And treasure my commands within you,
So that you incline your ear to wisdom,
And apply your heart to understanding;
Yes, if you cry out for discernment,
And lift up your voice for understanding,
If you seek her as silver,

And search for her as for hidden treasures;
Then you will understand the fear of the LORD,
And find the knowledge of God.
For the LORD *gives wisdom;*
From His mouth come knowledge and understanding;
He stores up sound wisdom for the upright;
He is a shield to those who walk uprightly;
He guards the paths of justice,
And preserves the way of His saints."   (Proverbs 2:1–8)

Discretion from God

We are promised from the word of God that when wisdom does enter our heart, then discretion will preserve us, and understanding will keep us and deliver us from the way of evil:

"When wisdom enters your heart,
And knowledge is pleasant to your soul,
Discretion will preserve you;
Understanding will keep you,
To deliver you from the way of evil,
From the man who speaks perverse things."
                                          (Proverbs 2:10–12)

Confessing the word

Confession of the word of God plays an important part in our lives. There have been extremes of teaching on this subject but, as always in these matters, they contain an element of truth. When some people try to confess the word of God, they expect it to work in a mechanical manner. We must always remember that it is our faith in Jesus Christ which is most important of all and, as we believe in Him and have our spiritual eyes fixed entirely on Him, then when we come to speak out the word of God, the Holy Spirit will guide us into all truth.

He will give us guidance concerning the scriptures we should confess in the circumstances we encounter. Scripture says:

"Death and life are in the power of the tongue,
And those who love it will eat its fruit."   (Proverbs 18:21)

I have found that there is tremendous blessing in confessing the word of God at the right time and place. For example, when I have been ill I have found the following confession to be a very powerful one:

> *"I shall not die, but live,*
> *And declare the works of the* LORD.
> *The* LORD *has chastened me severely,*
> *But He has not given me over to death."*   (Psalm 118:17–18)

Similarly, in the deliverance ministry I have found that when we confess Psalm 18:1–6 and call upon the Lord, the power of God falls:

> *"To the Chief Musician. A Psalm of David the servant of the* LORD, *who spoke to the* LORD *the words of this song on the day that the* LORD *delivered him from the hand of all his enemies and from the hand of Saul. And he said:*
>
> *I will love You, O* LORD, *my strength.*
> *The* LORD *is my rock and my fortress and my deliverer;*
> *My God, my strength, in whom I will trust;*
> *My shield and the horn of my salvation, my stronghold.*
> *I will call upon the* LORD, *who is worthy to be praised;*
> *So shall I be saved from my enemies.*
> *The pangs of death encompassed me,*
> *And the floods of ungodliness made me afraid.*
> *The sorrows of Sheol surrounded me;*
> *The snares of death confronted me.*
> *In my distress I called upon the* LORD,
> *And cried out to my God;*
> *He heard my voice from His temple,*
> *And my cry came before Him, even to His ears."*
>
> (Psalm 18:1–6)

That is why Scripture gives us this promise:

> *"And it shall come to pass that whoever calls on the name of the Lord shall be saved."*   (Acts 2:21)

Calling upon the name of the Lord and confessing Scripture brings tremendous faith and power into every aspect of our life.

Summary

1. The word of God effectively works within and changes the lives of believers.

2. It provides guidance for every aspect of our life.

3. As we hold onto mercy and truth, we find favor and high esteem in the sight of God and man.

4. We should trust God with all our heart and not lean on our own understanding, then He will direct our paths.

5. As we honor the Lord with our possessions and give Him the firstfruits of all that He gives us, then we will be blessed.

6. The word of God is health to our flesh.

7. The word of God promises that, as we call upon God in the day of trouble, He will deliver us and we will glorify Him.

8. The word of God protects us and warns us against sin.

9. We should hide the word of God in our heart so that we will not sin against Him.

10. The word of God protects us from the paths of the destroyer.

11. The word of God grants us wisdom and discernment.

12. We are given discretion by the word of God. This discretion will preserve us and by understanding the word we will be kept away from evil.

13. As we confess the word of God with belief, our faith is increased. We are thereby blessed and delivered.

Chapter 5

Jesus the Author and Finisher of Our Faith

Jesus as the rock

The measure of our true faith is our faith in the Lord Jesus Christ.

When we come into full repentance and allow God to destroy the power of sin which has afflicted our lives and hindered our walk with Him, then Jesus Christ becomes a living reality in our lives.

This is when we are born again of the Spirit of God. Those who are truly born again of the Spirit of God have an immediate desire in their heart to witness to others about the goodness of God and especially about His Son, Jesus Christ.

We come at once into a personal relationship with Jesus Christ. We are sure of His existence, of the fact that He is alive and that He walks with us by His Holy Spirit. Jesus Christ is the foundation of our walk with God. We see this in 1 Peter 2:6:

> *"Therefore it is also contained in the Scripture,*
>
> > *'Behold, I lay in Zion*
> > *A chief cornerstone, elect, precious,*
> > *And he who believes on Him will by no means be put to shame.'"*

The chief cornerstone is Jesus Christ. It is not a church, it is not a person, it is not a denomination, it is Jesus Christ Himself. This is why Jesus said these words in Matthew 16:18:

"And I also say to you that you are Peter, and on this rock I will build My church, and the gates of Hades shall not prevail against it."

Having used Peter's name, in Greek *Petros*, which means "a small stone or pebble," He then uses the word for "rock," *petra*. He is comparing Peter as a small pebble to Himself as a large rock or cornerstone. Many scriptures confirm that Jesus is the Rock, for example:

"He is the Rock, His work is perfect;
For all His ways are justice,
A God of truth and without injustice;
Righteous and upright is He." (Deuteronomy 32:4)

Jesus as the rock, fortress and deliverer

"The LORD is my rock and my fortress and my deliverer;
My God, my strength, in whom I will trust;
My shield and the horn of my salvation, my stronghold."
(Psalm 18:2)

One of the clearest scriptures which speaks of Jesus as the Rock is 1 Corinthians 10:4:

"and all drank the same spiritual drink. For they drank of that spiritual Rock that followed them, and that Rock was Christ."

Jesus the author and finisher of our faith

We should never have faith in faith itself. Our faith must be in Jesus Christ. This is why Scripture says:

"looking unto Jesus, the author and finisher of our faith, who for the joy that was set before Him endured the cross, despising the shame, and has sat down at the right hand of the throne of God." (Hebrews 12:2)

Our faith must be based entirely in Jesus Christ. He gives us our faith when we are born again. It is by faith in Him that we are born again. As we continue to walk with Him and read the word of God, then our faith grows. This should be a daily walk with God.

The reality of Jesus

When we are drawn by the Holy Spirit into true salvation, a spiritual transaction takes place and our hearts become convinced of the certainty of the reality of Jesus Christ. This certainty is just as sure as that which was in the heart of the Apostle John when he wrote his first epistle:

> *"the life was manifested, and we have seen, and bear witness, and declare to you that eternal life which was with the Father and was manifested to us – that which we have seen and heard we declare to you, that you also may have fellowship with us; and truly our fellowship is with the Father and with His Son Jesus Christ."* (1 John 1:2–3)

This same certainty is evident throughout all the writings of Peter, Paul and John. For example, Peter says in Acts 3:13–16:

> *"The God of Abraham, Isaac, and Jacob, the God of our fathers, glorified His Servant Jesus, whom you delivered up and denied in the presence of Pilate, when he was determined to let Him go. But you denied the Holy One and the Just, and asked for a murderer to be granted to you, and killed the Prince of life, whom God raised from the dead, of which we are witnesses. And His name, through faith in His name, has made this man strong, whom you see and know. Yes, the faith which comes through Him has given him this perfect soundness in the presence of you all."*

And Paul declares in his second letter to Timothy:

> *"For this reason I also suffer these things; nevertheless I am not ashamed, for I know whom I have believed and am persuaded that He is able to keep what I have committed to Him until that Day."* (2 Timothy 1:12)

Ever since I was born again, I have had the same certainty in my own heart, that as we surrender ourselves and totally yield to the Lordship of Jesus Christ, then His reality comes into our life. One of the scriptures which has greatly blessed me in this regard is Acts 2:25:

> *"For David says concerning Him:*
>
> > *'I foresaw the LORD always before my face, For He is at my right hand, that I may not be shaken.'"*

I well recall a healing miracle which took place in Wellington, New Zealand, some years ago. While I was praying for an elderly man who had arthritis in his hands, suddenly his wife began to scream. I asked her what was the matter. She cried out, "Don't you see them, don't you see them?" I said I did not see anything. She said, "As you are laying your hands on my husband's hands, I see the nail-printed hands of Jesus over your hands."

Yes, Jesus Christ is just as close to us as this. By the Holy Spirit, He is always walking before us and beside us. He walks before us to prepare the way and beside us to encourage us and to speak to us. We have the promise of Jesus Himself concerning the Holy Spirit:

> *"However, when He, the Spirit of truth, has come, He will guide you into all truth; for He will not speak on His own authority, but whatever He hears He will speak; and He will tell you things to come."*   (John 16:13)

Jesus promises never to leave us nor forsake us

> *"I will never leave you nor forsake you."*   (Hebrews 13:5)

Let us have the certainty of God's love in our hearts

Let us walk with that certainty in our heart at all times. As we take hold of these promises of God and let them grow in our lives, the reality of Jesus Christ will always be apparent.

Whenever I am ministering, I always believe in the abiding presence of God with me. As I listen to His voice very quickly the Lord begins to give me words of knowledge and also guides me in the leadership of the meeting. As I listen to Him, I find that, in fact, the words of knowledge are correct. Many people come forward for salvation, miracles of healing and deliverance occur, and the anointing of God falls upon them.

Yes, never let us forget, Jesus has promised never to leave us nor forsake us.

Summary

1. Jesus is the rock of our salvation. He is the chief cornerstone. It is not a church, or a person, or a denomination, but Jesus Christ Himself who is the rock.

2. He is our fortress and our deliverer.

3. He is the author and finisher of our faith. Our faith must be centered entirely in Jesus Christ.

4. When we are born again of the Spirit of God, the reality of Jesus Christ becomes a certainty in our hearts. He becomes absolutely real to us.

5. Jesus promises never to leave nor forsake us.

6. We should know the certainty of God's love in our hearts.

Chapter 6

Continuing to Walk in Faith

Living by faith

The prophet Habakkuk says:

> *"Behold the proud,*
> *His soul is not upright in him;*
> *But the just shall live by his faith."* (Habakkuk 2:4)

The words "just" and "righteous" are interchangeable. It is noteworthy that this scripture is quoted on three occasions in the New Testament, twice by Paul:

> *"For in it the righteousness of God is revealed from faith to faith;*
> *as it is written, 'The just shall live by faith.'"* (Romans 1:17)

> *"But that no one is justified by the law in the sight of God is*
> *evident, for 'The just shall live by faith.'"* (Galatians 3:11)

> *"Now the just shall live by faith;*
> *But if anyone draws back,*
> *My soul has no pleasure in him."* (Hebrews 10:38)

Living by faith covers every aspect of our lives: whether we are eating or sleeping, or speaking, or whatever we are doing, we should be living this life by faith in Jesus Christ.

When we are truly born again, every aspect of our life should be directed and governed by the Spirit of God through faith in Jesus Christ. We are justified by our faith in Jesus Christ, not by our works. However, good works should follow our faith.

Warning: believing in vain

Paul has warned us that we can believe in vain:

> *"by which also you are saved, if you hold fast that word which I preached to you – unless you believed in vain."*
>
> (1 Corinthians 15:2)

Some people believe that once we receive the gift of salvation, we will remain always saved no matter what we do. This is not a correct interpretation of Scripture.

Scripture says:

> *"Therefore consider the goodness and severity of God: on those who fell, severity; but toward you, goodness, if you continue in His goodness. Otherwise you also will be cut off."*
>
> (Romans 11:22)

We need to continue in the goodness of God. It is true that the gifts and calling of God are irrevocable.

> *"For the gifts and the calling of God are irrevocable."*
>
> (Romans 11:29)

We must understand that God does not take away from us the gift of salvation. However, we can elect to walk away from it because of disobedience toward God. That is why God says we will be judged by the fruit of our lives:

> *"Beware of false prophets, who come to you in sheep's clothing, but inwardly they are ravenous wolves. You will know them by their fruits. Do men gather grapes from thornbushes or figs from thistles? Even so, every good tree bears good fruit, but a bad tree bears bad fruit. A good tree cannot bear bad fruit, nor can a bad tree bear good fruit. Every tree that does not bear good fruit is cut down and thrown into the fire. Therefore by their fruits you will know them. Not everyone who says to Me, 'Lord, Lord,' shall enter the kingdom of heaven, but he who does the will of My Father in heaven. Many will say to Me in that day, 'Lord, Lord, have we not prophesied in Your name, cast out demons in Your name, and done many wonders in Your name?' And then I will declare to them, 'I never knew you; depart from Me, you who practice lawlessness!'"*   (Matthew 7:15–23)

Those who do the works of God

Jesus commends those who not only hear His words but do them:

> *"Therefore whoever hears these sayings of Mine, and does them, I will liken him to a wise man who built his house on the rock."*
> (Matthew 7:24)

Result of disobedience

In 1 Corinthians 10, we are given a warning about those who previously drank at the spiritual rock of Jesus Christ but, because of disobedience, were destroyed:

> *"Moreover, brethren, I do not want you to be unaware that all our fathers were under the cloud, all passed through the sea, all were baptized into Moses in the cloud and in the sea, all ate the same spiritual food, and all drank the same spiritual drink. For they drank of that spiritual Rock that followed them, and that Rock was Christ. But with most of them God was not well pleased, for their bodies were scattered in the wilderness. Now these things became our examples, to the intent that we should not lust after evil things as they also lusted. And do not become idolaters as were some of them. As it is written, 'The people sat down to eat and drink, and rose up to play.' Nor let us commit sexual immorality, as some of them did, and in one day twenty-three thousand fell; nor let us tempt Christ, as some of them also tempted, and were destroyed by serpents; nor complain, as some of them also complained, and were destroyed by the destroyer. Now all these things happened to them as examples, and they were written for our admonition, upon whom the ends of the ages have come. Therefore let him who thinks he stands take heed lest he fall."* (1 Corinthians 10:1–12)

Help from God

However, God does make it clear in His word that the temptations which face us are common to all human beings and that He will not allow us to be tempted more than we can bear. He will provide a way of escape to enable us to bear the temptation:

> *"No temptation has overtaken you except such as is common to man; but God is faithful, who will not allow you to be tempted*

beyond what you are able, but with the temptation will also make the way of escape, that you may be able to bear it."

(1 Corinthians 10:13)

The discipline of God

There are times when God needs to chasten us for our own good, and this is, in fact, a sign of His love for us:

"And you have forgotten the exhortation which speaks to you as to sons:

'My son, do not despise the chastening of the LORD,
Nor be discouraged when you are rebuked by Him ... ' "

(Hebrews 12:5)

This is the way a true human father deals with his son. If God did not chasten us, we would be illegitimate and not sons:

"If you endure chastening, God deals with you as with sons; for what son is there whom a father does not chasten? But if you are without chastening, of which all have become partakers, then you are illegitimate and not sons. Furthermore, we have had human fathers who corrected us, and we paid them respect. Shall we not much more readily be in subjection to the Father of spirits and live? For they indeed for a few days chastened us as seemed best to them, but He for our profit, that we may be partakers of His holiness. Now no chastening seems to be joyful for the present, but painful; nevertheless, afterward it yields the peaceable fruit of righteousness to those who have been trained by it."

(Hebrews 12:7–11)

Deliberate sin

When we are tempted, we can turn to God through Jesus Christ. As we truly repent and stand firm against that temptation He will make a way of escape for us. However, if we continuously succumb and turn away into deliberate sin, then Hebrews 10:26–30 tells us what we can expect:

"For if we sin willfully after we have received the knowledge of the truth, there no longer remains a sacrifice for sins, but a certain fearful expectation of judgment, and fiery indignation which will devour the adversaries. Anyone who has rejected Moses' law dies without mercy on the testimony of two or three

witnesses. Of how much worse punishment, do you suppose, will he be thought worthy who has trampled the Son of God under-foot, counted the blood of the covenant by which he was sanctified a common thing, and insulted the Spirit of grace? For we know Him who said, 'Vengeance is Mine, I will repay,' says the Lord. And again, 'The LORD will judge His people.'"

(Hebrews 10:26–30)

Deliverance from temptations

Whenever we are tempted and turn to God, He will always help us because He knows how to deliver us:

> *"then the Lord knows how to deliver the godly out of temptations and to reserve the unjust under punishment for the day of judgment . . . "* (2 Peter 2:9)

Walking in holiness

We need to walk carefully before God in holiness and in true righteousness which come from God Himself:

> *"For the time has come for judgment to begin at the house of God; and if it begins with us first, what will be the end of those who do not obey the gospel of God? Now*
>
> *'If the righteous one is scarcely saved,*
> *Where will the ungodly and the sinner appear?'"*

(1 Peter 4:17–18)

Pardon from sin

We must always remember, however, that God is open to pardon and forgive us if we do fall into sin:

> *"If we confess our sins, He is faithful and just to forgive us our sins and to cleanse us from all unrighteousness."* (1 John 1:9)

If we do fall into sin, it is good for us to confess it to others, particularly the elders of our church, and come into the forgiveness that God offers.

However, confessing our sins should not become the easy way out. We should not confess our sins one day and go and do the same sin the next day. This is not walking in true repentance.

If we want to receive the best from God, then we must give Him of our best.

Let us always remember that the Lord is gracious and long-suffering and will always forgive us when we come to Him with a penitent heart. We can all make mistakes, but if we truly turn back to the Lord with all our heart, then we will find He is always gracious to forgive.

However, Scripture says that the Day of the Lord will come like a thief in the night and we should always be prepared to meet God face to face and, therefore, we should not continue in deliberate sin.

Results of obedience

As we do, in fact, seek to obey God, then our faith toward Him grows day by day. Our great example in faith is Abraham. Scripture says about him:

> *"For what does the Scripture say? 'Abraham believed God, and it was accounted to him for righteousness.'"*   (Romans 4:3)

> *"And not being weak in faith, he did not consider his own body, already dead (since he was about a hundred years old), and the deadness of Sarah's womb. He did not waver at the promise of God through unbelief, but was strengthened in faith, giving glory to God, and being fully convinced that what He had promised He was also able to perform."*   (Romans 4:19–21)

God promises Abraham many descendants

On an occasion when God revealed Himself to him, Abram, as he was still called, complained to God that, since he had no offspring and was without an heir, Eliezer of Damascus would become his heir. But God promised he would indeed have an heir:

> *"And behold, the word of the LORD came to him, saying, 'This one shall not be your heir, but one who will come from your own body shall be your heir.'"*   (Genesis 15:4)

Then, taking him outside his tent, God told him to look at the skies and see if he could count the stars. Obviously Abraham couldn't, but then the word of God came to him again:

> *"'So shall your descendants be.' And he believed in the* LORD *and He accounted it to him for righteousness."*
>
> (Genesis 15:5–6)

Even though Abraham was ninety-nine years old, Scripture says:

> *"And not being weak in faith, he did not consider his own body, already dead (since he was about a hundred years old), and the deadness of Sarah's womb. He did not waver at the promise of God through unbelief, but was strengthened in faith, giving glory to God, and being fully convinced that what He had promised He was also able to perform."* (Romans 4:19–21)

Because Abram believed God, he was told that he would be a father of many nations and God changed his name to Abraham.

> *"No longer shall your name be called Abram, but your name shall be Abraham; for I have made you a father of many nations."* (Genesis 17:5)

It was accounted to Abraham as righteousness

Just as, because Abraham believed the word of God, it was accounted to him as righteousness, so we are told that, in the same way, righteousness will be accounted to us if we believe in Him who raised up Jesus our Lord from the dead.

Thus, God gives us a gift of faith to believe in Him, but then He wants us to continue to believe and act upon that belief.

Many people try to earn their salvation. This is impossible. If we could work our way into heaven by our good deeds alone, then it would not have been necessary for Jesus Christ to have come to this earth and died a cruel death on the cross in order to pay the penalty for our sins. No, we cannot earn our salvation by good works. Salvation is a gift from God and we are required to believe in our heart and confess with our mouth that Jesus Christ has been raised from the dead.

As the scripture says:

> *"But we are all like an unclean thing,*
> *And all our righteousnesses are like filthy rags;*
> *We all fade as a leaf,*
> *And our iniquities, like the wind,*
> *Have taken us away."* (Isaiah 64:6)

Thus, our own works or righteous acts will not save us. Saving faith comes from God Himself as we believe absolutely in the name of His Son, Jesus Christ.

Summary

1. We are justified by faith. *"The just shall live by his faith."* Every aspect of our lives should be governed by faith in Jesus Christ.

2. If we do not continue to obey God, then we can believe in vain.

3. The wise person builds his or her house on the rock by being obedient to Jesus.

4. Disobedience to God results in destruction.

5. God will help us in times of trial.

6. Just as a natural father disciplines his own children in love, so God disciplines us for our own good.

7. We should avoid deliberate sin at all costs.

8. If we turn to God, He will deliver us from sin.

9. God will pardon and forgive us if we turn back to Him in true repentance.

10. Just as it was accounted to Abraham as righteousness when he believed God, similarly, righteousness will be accounted to us if we believe in Him who raised up Jesus our Lord from the dead.

Chapter 7

Faith and Works

Many Christians place such an emphasis on faith that they overlook what the word of God has to say concerning works. It is important that we seek the whole truth of God from His word so that we have a balanced walk with Him. We must understand exactly what the word of God says concerning the place of works in the life of the Christian.

We are appointed for good works

> "For we are His workmanship, created in Christ Jesus for good works, which God prepared beforehand that we should walk in them."
> (Ephesians 2:10)

We are required to walk in these good works, having our total faith in Jesus Christ. We are not saved by our works but we are saved by faith in Jesus Christ and our works should follow.

Works follow faith

We must clearly understand the place of works in relation to our faith. Our good works should follow our faith in Jesus. Our righteous acts, that is our own attempts to obtain right standing with God by our own efforts rather than through Jesus Christ, are like filthy rags.

> "But we are all like an unclean thing,
> And all our righteousnesses are like filthy rags;
> We all fade as a leaf,
> And our iniquities, like the wind,
> Have taken us away."
> (Isaiah 64:6)

After we have committed our lives to Jesus Christ, then we should go on in good works, as directed by Scripture. These good works should follow our belief in Jesus Christ. As James says:

> *"Pure and undefiled religion before God and the Father is this: to visit orphans and widows in their trouble, and to keep oneself unspotted from the world."*   (James 1:27)

Faith without works is dead

James makes the point very clearly that faith by itself, if it does not have works, is dead.

> *"Thus also faith by itself, if it does not have works, is dead."*
> (James 2:17)

He goes on to challenge the person who asserts, *"You have faith and I have works."* He says, *"Show me your faith without your works and I will show my faith by my works."*

He does not end the challenge there, however. He points out that, even though the demons have faith in God, their faith is insufficient for their salvation.

> *"You believe that there is one God. You do well. Even the demons believe – and tremble!"*   (James 2:19)

Abraham was instructed by God to offer his only son, Isaac, whom he loved, as a burnt offering on one of the mountains in the land of Moriah. Abraham didn't argue with God. He simply obeyed Him. When he came near the place where God had told him to sacrifice his son, he instructed the other young men with him to stay with the donkey while he and Isaac went ahead to worship God. Then they would return.

Abraham had such faith that, even though God told him to kill his own son, he still believed that God would raise Isaac from the dead. God was testing him.

After he had bound his son and laid him on the wood, he stretched out his hand with the knife ready to kill him. It was at that moment that the angel of the Lord called from heaven and said, *"Abraham, Abraham"*, and he said, *"Here I am."*

The Lord then said to him:

> *"Do not lay your hand on the lad, or do anything to him; for now I know that you fear God, since you have not withheld your son, your only son, from Me."* (Genesis 22:12)

Abraham then sacrificed a ram, which he found caught in the thicket by its horns, in the place of Isaac.

Because Abraham did works, that is obeyed God and carried out what God told him to do, then God promised him great blessings as a result of his faith and obedience.

> *"Then the Angel of the LORD called to Abraham a second time out of heaven, and said: 'By Myself I have sworn, says the LORD, because you have done this thing, and have not withheld your son, your only son, in blessing I will bless you, and in multiplying I will multiply your descendants as the stars of the heaven and as the sand which is on the seashore; and your descendants shall possess the gate of their enemies. In your seed all the nations of the earth shall be blessed, because you have obeyed My voice.' "* (Genesis 22:15–18)

In that way, the faith of Abraham was working alongside his works and, by those works, his faith was made perfect. We find throughout the New Testament a continuous emphasis upon works following faith. For example, when Paul was speaking to the elders of the church from Ephesus, he said:

> *"I have shown you in every way, by laboring like this, that you must support the weak. And remember the words of the Lord Jesus, that He said, 'It is more blessed to give than to receive.' "* (Acts 20:35)

Paul commends works

Paul commends the churches of Macedonia for their abundance in giving:

> *"that in a great trial of affliction the abundance of their joy and their deep poverty abounded in the riches of their liberality."* (2 Corinthians 8:2)

Letter to the Galatians
In his letter to the Galatians he refers again to the poor:

> *"They desired only that we should remember the poor, the very thing which I also was eager to do."* (Galatians 2:10)

Letter to the Philippians

He commends the Philippian church for their gift to him:

> *"For even in Thessalonica you sent aid once and again for my necessities. Not that I seek the gift, but I seek the fruit that abounds to your account. Indeed I have all and abound. I am full, having received from Epaphroditus the things sent from you, a sweet-smelling aroma, an acceptable sacrifice, well pleasing to God."*   (Philippians 4:16–18)

Second letter to the Thessalonians

In his second letter to the Thessalonians, Paul counsels the church not to grow weary in doing good:

> *"But as for you, brethren, do not grow weary in doing good."*
>   (2 Thessalonians 3:13)

First letter to Timothy

In his first letter to Timothy, Paul speaks of good works in relation to widows:

> *"Do not let a widow under sixty years old be taken into the number, and not unless she has been the wife of one man, well reported for good works: if she has brought up children, if she has lodged strangers, if she has washed the saints' feet, if she has relieved the afflicted, if she has diligently followed every good work."*   (1 Timothy 5:9–10)

Paul also tells us that those who do not provide for their own and especially for their own household, have denied the faith and are worse than an unbeliever:

> *"But if anyone does not provide for his own, and especially for those of his household, he has denied the faith and is worse than an unbeliever."*   (1 Timothy 5:8)

He also commands the rich to do good:

> *"Let them do good, that they be rich in good works, ready to give, willing to share, storing up for themselves a good foundation for the time to come, that they may lay hold on eternal life."*
>   (1 Timothy 6:18–19)

Letter to Titus

Paul encourages Titus to be an example to others by doing good works:

> *"in all things showing yourself to be a pattern of good works; in doctrine showing integrity, reverence, incorruptibility."*
>
> (Titus 2:7)

He reminds us that Jesus wants a special people, who are zealous to do good works.

> *"who gave Himself for us, that He might redeem us from every lawless deed and purify for Himself His own special people, zealous for good works."* (Titus 2:14)

These good works should be a constant feature of not only his own life but of all those who profess to believe in God:

> *"This is a faithful saying, and these things I want you to affirm constantly, that those who have believed in God should be careful to maintain good works. These things are good and profitable to men."* (Titus 3:8)

> *"And let our people also learn to maintain good works, to meet urgent needs, that they may not be unfruitful."* (Titus 3:14)

Letter to the Hebrews

The writer of Hebrews also urges:

> *"And let us consider one another in order to stir up love and good works,"* (Hebrews 10:24)

The Apostle John commends works

The Apostle John reminds us of the need to show our love by our works:

> *"But whoever has this world's goods, and sees his brother in need, and shuts up his heart from him, how does the love of God abide in him? My little children, let us not love in word or in tongue, but in deed and in truth."* (1 John 3:17–18)

Jesus and works

Matthew 25 contains a very solemn warning to all Christians, setting out clearly the judgment that will take place in connection with everyone's works.

Jesus describes the judgment, when He will sit on the throne of His glory and everybody will be gathered before Him. Then He will separate the sheep from the goats on the basis of works. In this chapter He identifies six groups of people as His "brethren," namely the hungry, the thirsty, the stranger, the naked, the sick and those in prison. The word "brethren" is used here with the same wide meaning as He gives to the words "mother and brothers" in the following verses from Luke:

> *"And it was told Him by some, who said, 'Your mother and Your brothers are standing outside, desiring to see You.' But He answered and said to them, 'My mother and My brothers are these who hear the word of God and do it.'"* (Luke 8:20–21)

Similarly, we learn from the parable of the good Samaritan, in Luke 10:30–37, that our neighbor is anybody who is in need. In this well-known story a man, who is on a journey from Jerusalem to Jericho, falls among thieves, who strip him of his clothing, wound him and depart leaving him half dead. Jesus tells how a priest passes by on the other side of the road, ignoring the wounded man's plight. A while later a Levite does exactly the same. But a Samaritan, when he sees the man, has compassion on him and bandages his wounds, pouring on oil and wine, and carries him on his animal to an inn where he takes care of him. The next day he gives the innkeeper money with instructions to continue to care for the man.

Then Jesus says:

> *" 'So which of these three do you think was neighbor to him who fell among the thieves?' And he said, 'He who showed mercy on him.' Then Jesus said to him, 'Go and do likewise.'"*
> (Luke 10:36–37)

Thus, from this parable we learn that the term "neighbor" as used by Jesus has a much wider application than its normal use. Similarly, the word "brethren" is used in Luke 8:20–21 above in a wider context than we would normally attribute to it.

Turning now to what Jesus says about how He will judge humankind:

> *"When the Son of Man comes in His glory, and all the holy angels with Him, then He will sit on the throne of His glory. All*

*the nations will be gathered before Him, and He will separate
them one from another, as a shepherd divides his sheep from the
goats. And He will set the sheep on His right hand, but the goats
on the left. Then the King will say to those on His right hand,
'Come, you blessed of My Father, inherit the kingdom prepared
for you from the foundation of the world: for I was hungry and
you gave Me food; I was thirsty and you gave Me drink; I was a
stranger and you took Me in; I was naked and you clothed Me; I
was sick and you visited Me; I was in prison and you came to
Me.' Then the righteous will answer Him, saying, 'Lord, when
did we see You hungry and feed You, or thirsty and give You
drink? When did we see You a stranger and take You in, or
naked and clothe You? Or when did we see You sick, or in prison,
and come to You?' And the King will answer and say to them,
'Assuredly, I say to you, inasmuch as you did it to one of the
least of these My brethren, you did it to Me.'*

*"Then He will also say to those on the left hand, 'Depart from
Me, you cursed, into the everlasting fire prepared for the devil
and his angels: for I was hungry and you gave Me no food; I was
thirsty and you gave Me no drink; I was a stranger and you did
not take Me in, naked and you did not clothe Me, sick and in
prison and you did not visit Me.' Then they also will answer
Him, saying, 'Lord, when did we see You hungry or thirsty or
a stranger or naked or sick or in prison, and did not minister
to You?' Then He will answer them, saying, 'Assuredly, I say to
you, inasmuch as you did not do it to one of the least of these,
you did not do it to Me.' And these will go away into everlasting
punishment, but the righteous into eternal life."*

(Matthew 25:31–46)

Jesus identifies the sheep as those who will inherit the kingdom
of God because they took care of the hungry, the thirsty, the
stranger, the naked, the sick and those in prison. These are the
good works that should follow our salvation in Jesus Christ.

Then Jesus goes on to identify those on his left hand, the
"goats," and says these words:

*"Depart from Me, you cursed, into the everlasting fire prepared
for the devil and his angels ... "* (Matthew 25:41)

These are the people who have not helped the brethren of Jesus,
namely the hungry, the thirsty, the stranger, the naked, the sick

or in prison. Jesus says that these will be sent into everlasting punishment, but the righteous into eternal life.

We need to understand clearly that the use of the word "brethren" above does not mean these people are the sons and daughters of God. Unless they too come to Jesus Christ as Lord and Savior and are born again, then they remain unsaved. However, it may well be that as a result of our care of them they will turn back to the Lord.

Some years ago, when visiting Ethiopia where I saw many people starving as a result of the terrible droughts, the Lord illuminated this scripture to me in a particular way. It was only the work of Christian organizations like World Vision that was saving the lives of these people. Many Muslims were among those who were being helped.

At that time it was impossible to preach the gospel of Jesus Christ in Ethiopia since the Communist Government would not allow it.

When, some years later, a representative of World Vision returned to Ethiopia, he found many of the Muslims had turned to Jesus Christ. They had witnessed the love of God exhibited through the Christians working with World Vision and experienced the help given to them in the supply of food to prevent their starvation. As a result of the love of Jesus through the World Vision workers they were saved, even though no outsider had preached the gospel to them. A seed had been sown in their hearts through the concern of those who had taken care of them.

The observer from World Vision found that many churches were functioning in an area formerly largely Muslim. These people had come to the Lord solely because of the help being given to them through World Vision. As a result of the seed which had been sown in their hearts, the few Christians in the area were able to tell the Muslims about Jesus and that is why many had turned to the Lord.

In many Islamic countries today it is forbidden to preach the gospel. The only way we can proclaim the gospel of Jesus Christ is by helping the hungry, the thirsty, the stranger, the naked, the sick and those in prison. As we show the love of Jesus to them, many will of their own accord turn to the Lord.

This, of course, is in total accord with the word of God which tells us that all the commandments are summed up in one saying, namely, *"You shall love your neighbor as yourself."*

As we love those in need (our neighbors), regardless of their spiritual understanding, then we are acting in obedience to the word of God in a practical way. God is able to speak to their hearts through us and draw them to Jesus Christ.

> *"For the commandments, 'You shall not commit adultery,' 'You shall not murder,' 'You shall not steal,' 'You shall not bear false witness,' 'You shall not covet,' and if there is any other commandment, are all summed up in this saying, namely, 'You shall love your neighbor as yourself.' Love does no harm to a neighbor; therefore love is the fulfillment of the law."*
> (Romans 13:9–10)

Reward according to works

Jesus has said that when He returns, He will reward each one of His followers according to his or her works.

> *"For the Son of Man will come in the glory of His Father with His angels, and then He will reward each according to his works."*
> (Matthew 16:27)

Summing up, therefore, we conclude that there is no contradiction between what Paul and James are saying. Paul emphasizes both the fact that we are justified by faith and that we should maintain good works. James points out that belief and faith are not enough because even the demons have faith in God and believe in Him. Our works must follow our faith, otherwise faith without works is dead.

Summary

1. We are created in Christ Jesus for good works.

2. If our faith is firmly centered in Jesus Christ, then our faith should result in good works.

3. Faith without works is dead.

4. As Abraham exercised his faith in God and carried out God's commands, his faith was made perfect.

5. The Apostle Paul commends the good works of the churches of Macedonia, the Galatians and the Philippians. He also encourages the Thessalonians not to grow weary in doing good.

6. Paul tells the rich to do good and reminds us that we should be zealous in doing good works. He also urges Titus to maintain those good works.

7. The Apostle John reminds us of the need to show our love by good works.

8. Jesus clearly states the need to take care of the hungry, the thirsty, the stranger, the naked, the sick and those in prison.

9. By helping these people we can, in fact, proclaim the gospel of Jesus Christ. The commandments are summed up in this saying, *"You shall love your neighbor as yourself."*

10. On His return, Jesus will reward each person according to his or her works.

Chapter 8

Understanding God's Unmerited Favor or Grace

God's law

God's divine system of law was given by Him to Moses and can be found in the books of Exodus, Leviticus, Numbers and Deuteronomy. Perhaps the most well-known part of the law of Moses is known as the Ten Commandments, set out in Exodus 20:1–17.

In addition to the Ten Commandments, the law covered such aspects as dietary requirements, the offering of sacrifices, laws concerning violence, control of animals, responsibility for property, dealing with sorcery, justice, Sabbath regulations, and offerings at the temple including grain offerings, peace offerings, sin offerings, burnt offerings and trespass offerings. It set out the ritual to be followed after childbirth, the laws concerning leprosy, laws of sexual morality, the sanctity of blood, the conduct of priests, and feasts of the Lord such as the Sabbath, the Passover, the Feast of Firstfruits, the Feast of Weeks and the Day of Atonement, as well as the Feast of Tabernacles.

Banishment of Jews

The failure of the Jews to obey God and keep the law resulted in their banishment to Babylon. God clearly spelled out the blessings which He offered to those who were obedient to the law, as well as the curses which followed disobedience. Examples of these curses are as follows:

> '"But if you do not obey Me, and do not observe all these commandments, and if you despise My statutes, or if your soul

abhors My judgments, so that you do not perform all My commandments, but break My covenant, I also will do this to you: I will even appoint terror over you, wasting disease and fever which shall consume the eyes and cause sorrow of heart. And you shall sow your seed in vain, for your enemies shall eat it. I will set My face against you, and you shall be defeated by your enemies. Those who hate you shall reign over you, and you shall flee when no one pursues you."   (Leviticus 26:14–17)

"But it shall come to pass, if you do not obey the voice of the LORD *your God, to observe carefully all His commandments and His statutes which I command you today, that all these curses will come upon you and overtake you: Cursed shall you be in the city, and cursed shall you be in the country. Cursed shall be your basket and your kneading bowl. Cursed shall be the fruit of your body and the produce of your land, the increase of your cattle and the offspring of your flocks. Cursed shall you be when you come in, and cursed shall you be when you go out. The* LORD *will send on you cursing, confusion, and rebuke in all that you set your hand to do, until you are destroyed and until you perish quickly, because of the wickedness of your doings in which you have forsaken Me."*   (Deuteronomy 28:15–20)

Failure to keep one requirement of the law meant that you were guilty of breaking it all. This is set out in James 2:10–11:

"For whoever shall keep the whole law, and yet stumble in one point, he is guilty of all. For He who said, 'Do not commit adultery,' also said, 'Do not murder.' Now if you do not commit adultery, but you do murder, you have become a transgressor of the law."

Paul also makes the same point in Galatians 3:10:

"For as many as are of the works of the law are under the curse; for it is written, 'Cursed is everyone who does not continue in all things which are written in the book of the law, to do them.'"

It is therefore necessary for anyone who wants to keep the law of Moses to keep it in every respect, otherwise that person will come under the curse of God.

This system of divine law was given to God's chosen people, the Israelites, through His servant Moses. Because of their disobedience, the Jews were banished from the Promised Land for seventy years. Although under the leadership of Ezra and

Nehemiah they returned to the Promised Land, nevertheless the Jews never again regained the glory of their former kingdoms.

New covenant

God later promised that He would make a new covenant with the house of Israel and with the house of Judah:

> *"Behold, the days are coming, says the LORD, when I will make a new covenant with the house of Israel and with the house of Judah – not according to the covenant that I made with their fathers in the day that I took them by the hand to lead them out of the land of Egypt, My covenant which they broke, though I was a husband to them, says the LORD. But this is the covenant that I will make with the house of Israel after those days, says the LORD: I will put My law in their minds, and write it on their hearts; and I will be their God, and they shall be My people. No more shall every man teach his neighbor, and every man his brother, saying, 'Know the LORD,' for they all shall know Me, from the least of them to the greatest of them, says the LORD. For I will forgive their iniquity, and their sin I will remember no more."* (Jeremiah 31:31–34)

This new covenant, which replaced the old covenant, is available to everybody. Jesus Christ died for us all and anyone can come into the new covenant, by placing their faith in Jesus Christ.

> *"For God so loved the world that He gave His only begotten Son, that whoever believes in Him should not perish but have everlasting life."* (John 3:16)

The Mediator of this new covenant, that is the person who reconciles us to God, is Jesus Christ.

> *"But now He has obtained a more excellent ministry, inasmuch as He is also Mediator of a better covenant, which was established on better promises."* (Hebrews 8:6)

Grace and truth

With the coming of Jesus has dawned the era of grace and truth. "Grace" here means God's unmerited favor. We do not deserve this favor, but He has given it to us through His Son, Jesus Christ.

> *"For the law was given through Moses, but grace and truth came through Jesus Christ."*   (John 1:17)

This is confirmed in Romans 6:

> *"For sin shall not have dominion over you, for you are not under law but under grace."*   (Romans 6:14)

Paul preaching at Antioch

At Antioch Paul preached that our justification through Jesus Christ is complete:

> *"Therefore let it be known to you, brethren, that through this Man is preached to you the forgiveness of sins; and by Him everyone who believes is justified from all things from which you could not be justified by the law of Moses."*   (Acts 13:38–39)

Council of Jerusalem

In the early Church there was conflict over the question of whether the Gentiles were required to keep the law. Some who belonged to the sect of the Pharisees said that it was necessary to circumcise them and to command them to keep the law of Moses. After discussion, this Council agreed with James who said that the Gentiles should not be required to keep the law, but only to abstain from things polluted by idols, from sexual immorality, from eating animals which had been strangled and from blood. Subsequently the apostles and elders, with the whole Church, agreed and sent a letter via Paul and Barnabas and other leading men to the Gentiles in Antioch, Syria and Cilicia saying:

> *"Since we have heard that some who went out from us have troubled you with words, unsettling your souls, saying, 'You must be circumcised and keep the law' – to whom we gave no such commandment – it seemed good to us, being assembled with one accord, to send chosen men to you with our beloved Barnabas and Paul, men who have risked their lives for the name of our Lord Jesus Christ. We have therefore sent Judas and Silas, who will also report the same things by word of mouth. For*

it seemed good to the Holy Spirit, and to us, to lay upon you no greater burden than these necessary things: that you abstain from things offered to idols, from blood, from things strangled, and from sexual immorality. If you keep yourselves from these, you will do well. Farewell." (Acts 15:24–29)

Our deliverance from the law

In his preaching and teaching Paul tells us we are delivered from the law. He says that even though the law is holy and the commandments holy, just and good, nevertheless, sin, taking the opportunity afforded by the commandments of the law, produced in him all manner of evil desire (Romans 7:8). This is why Paul says in 1 Corinthians 15:56:

"The sting of death is sin, and the strength of sin is the law."

The more we try to keep the law, the more we become aware of sin within ourselves, exercising control over us even against our will.

When we put our faith in Jesus Christ, we no longer have to strive to keep the law, because now we have the Holy Spirit within us to help us live a holy life before God. That is why Paul is able to say:

"For Christ is the end of the law for righteousness to everyone who believes." (Romans 10:4)

Law remains

The law is not abolished or wiped out: as part of God's word, it will endure forever, but no longer do we obtain right standing with God by following the law, but rather by faith in Jesus Christ.

Jesus Christ has erased the record of the requirements of the law, which stood against us:

"having wiped out the handwriting of requirements that was against us, which was contrary to us. And He has taken it out of the way, having nailed it to the cross." (Colossians 2:14)

Because of this we are no longer subject to the judgment of others:

"So let no one judge you in food or in drink, or regarding a festival or a new moon or sabbaths ..." (Colossians 2:16)

He makes the point that these things were only a shadow of things to come, but the real substance is Christ:

"which are a shadow of things to come, but the substance is of Christ." (Colossians 2:17)

Although following the law is no longer the way to achieve salvation and although the law was given only to the Jews, nevertheless, its precepts still stand. For those Jews and Gentiles who fail to appropriate fully the work of the cross and Jesus Christ as Savior, the curse of the law can still apply. The curses set out in Deuteronomy 27 and 28 can still affect us. That is why, in his letter to the Galatians, who were Gentiles, Paul tells them:

"Christ has redeemed us from the curse of the law, having become a curse for us (for it is written, 'Cursed is everyone who hangs on a tree'), that the blessing of Abraham might come upon the Gentiles in Christ Jesus, that we might receive the promise of the Spirit through faith." (Galatians 3:13–14)

As we follow Jesus Christ and obey His word, we are delivered from that curse of the law. Obeying the law is no longer the means of achieving righteousness: it is by faith in Jesus Christ alone that we can be saved.

We follow Jesus

We are to keep our eyes on Jesus Christ and follow Him, not a set of legal requirements. As we follow and obey Jesus Christ, then we find God has put His righteousness in us through Jesus Christ.

It is through Jesus Christ that God has broken down the division between the Jew and Gentile. The law of Moses had added to that division.

"For He Himself is our peace, who has made both one, and has broken down the middle wall of separation, having abolished in His flesh the enmity, that is, the law of commandments contained in ordinances, so as to create in Himself one new man from the two, thus making peace, and that He might reconcile them both to God in one body through the cross, thereby putting to death the enmity." (Ephesians 2:14–16)

We are saved by grace, not the law

Thus, we have been saved by the grace of God, through faith, which is a gift of God:

> *"For by grace you have been saved through faith, and that not of yourselves; it is the gift of God, not of works, lest anyone should boast."*   (Ephesians 2:8–9)

Summing up, therefore, Paul again makes the position very clear when he says:

> *"But if you are led by the Spirit, you are not under the law."*   (Galatians 5:18)

The Holy Spirit guides us

We now have the Holy Spirit to guide us into all truth:

> *"However, when He, the Spirit of truth, has come, He will guide you into all truth; for He will not speak on His own authority, but whatever He hears He will speak; and He will tell you things to come."*   (John 16:13)

Of course, we must be certain that it is the Holy Spirit to whom we are listening. This will be confirmed or otherwise as we share in our understanding with other believers and as we submit to these other believers in Jesus Christ.

The difference between the new covenant and the old covenant

Under the old covenant, the Jews sought to establish their own righteousness, whereas under the new covenant, our righteousness is given to us by Jesus Christ.

> *"For they being ignorant of God's righteousness, and seeking to establish their own righteousness, have not submitted to the righteousness of God."*   (Romans 10:3)

Victory in Jesus

Summary

1. God gave a divine system of law to Moses which included the Ten Commandments. Those who disobeyed God's law came under His curse.

2. As a result of their disobedience to God, the Jews were banished to Babylon. They came under the curses of the law.

3. God promised He would make a new covenant with the house of Israel and the house of Judah.

4. This new covenant was confirmed in Jesus Christ by His atoning death on the cross and His resurrection.

5. Grace and truth came through the death and resurrection of Jesus Christ.

6. The Council of Jerusalem agreed that the Gentiles did not need to be circumcised and did not need to keep the law, but rather should abstain from things offered to idols, from blood, from eating animals which had been strangled and from sexual immorality.

7. The law remains a part of God's word.

8. We follow Jesus Christ, not a set of requirements.

9. We are saved by grace (God's unmerited favor to us) and not the law.

10. The Holy Spirit guides us.

11. Under the old covenant, the Jews sought to establish their own righteousness, whereas under the new covenant our righteousness is given to us by Jesus Christ.

12. Through the cross of Jesus Christ we are delivered from the curse of the law.

Chapter 9

The Reason God Gave the Law to Moses

Paul sets out the reasons why the law of Moses was given to the Jews.

The law was the tutor

"Is the law then against the promises of God? Certainly not! For if there had been a law given which could have given life, truly righteousness would have been by the law. But the Scripture has confined all under sin, that the promise by faith in Jesus Christ might be given to those who believe. But before faith came, we were kept under guard by the law, kept for the faith which would afterward be revealed. Therefore the law was our tutor to bring us to Christ, that we might be justified by faith. But after faith has come, we are no longer under a tutor."

(Galatians 3:21–25)

Paul is pointing out that before Jesus' atoning death and resurrection and before faith in Him was granted by God, the Jews were kept under the law, ready for the coming faith in Jesus Christ.

The law thus revealed to human beings their sinful state. Because they could not keep every exact part of the law, they could not make themselves righteous by their own efforts. The law also foreshadowed the coming Messiah, Jesus Christ, through whom salvation and righteousness would be given.

From these scriptures, we can see that the law brought the knowledge of sin and that it was intended to be a tutor to bring the Jews to Christ so that they could be justified by faith in Him.

After the death and resurrection of Jesus Christ, however, no one needs to be tutored by the law as a means to salvation.

The law brought a knowledge of sin

The law made human beings aware of their sinful condition. This is confirmed by the following scriptures:

> *"What shall we say then? Is the law sin? Certainly not! On the contrary, I would not have known sin except through the law. For I would not have known covetousness unless the law had said, 'You shall not covet.' But sin, taking opportunity by the commandment, produced in me all manner of evil desire. For apart from the law sin was dead. I was alive once without the law, but when the commandment came, sin revived and I died."*
> (Romans 7:7–9)

This purpose is further confirmed in the following scripture:

> *"Now we know that whatever the law says, it says to those who are under the law, that every mouth may be stopped, and all the world may become guilty before God. Therefore by the deeds of the law no flesh will be justified in His sight, for by the law is the knowledge of sin."*
> (Romans 3:19–20)

It showed human beings that they could not be made righteous by their own efforts

To their sorrow, the Israelites did not see Jesus Christ as the Messiah and as mediator of the new covenant. By the grace of God, however, many of the Gentiles have been given this knowledge of Jesus Christ. Paul compares the position of the Gentiles and the Israelites in the following scriptures:

> *"What shall we say then? That Gentiles, who did not pursue righteousness, have attained to righteousness, even the right-eousness of faith; but Israel, pursuing the law of righteousness, has not attained to the law of righteousness. Why? Because they did not seek it by faith, but as it were, by the works of the law. For they stumbled at that stumbling stone. As it is written:*
>
> > *'Behold, I lay in Zion a stumbling stone and rock of offense, And whoever believes on Him will not be put to shame.'"*
> (Romans 9:30–33)

No matter how hard we try, we cannot make ourselves righteous by our own efforts. This is what the religious Jews were trying to do but, of course, they failed.

Jesus as the Lamb of God

The law foreshadowed Jesus Christ as the coming Lamb of God.

The first seven chapters of Leviticus, which describe the sacrifices for sin and how the Israelites were to approach God, foreshadow the coming atoning death of Jesus Christ on the cross. That is why John the Baptist said about Jesus:

> *"The next day John saw Jesus coming toward him, and said, 'Behold! The Lamb of God who takes away the sin of the world!'"*
> (John 1:29)

Jesus Christ is the Lamb of sacrifice who takes away all of our sins. No longer are the sacrificial ordinances of the law necessary. However, most of the Jews did not accept this.

Christ fulfills the law

In His Sermon on the Mount, Jesus Christ made the following statements:

> *"Do not think that I came to destroy the Law or the Prophets. I did not come to destroy but to fulfill. For assuredly, I say to you, till heaven and earth pass away, one jot or one tittle will by no means pass from the law till all is fulfilled."* (Matthew 5:17–18)

Jesus Christ fulfilled the law in every respect, especially by His atoning death and resurrection through which we are made righteous. No longer do we have to follow the law in order to be made righteous before God.

Christ was born under the law

In accordance with the promise of God, Jesus was born of a woman under the law.

> *"But when the fullness of the time had come, God sent forth His Son, born of a woman, born under the law ..."*
> (Galatians 4:4)

Christ paid the penalty for sin

Jesus Christ has paid the full penalty required by the law for each of us; He has fulfilled all the requirements of the law. It is through Him and Him alone that we obtain righteousness before God.

Thus Paul was able to say in Romans 10:

> *"For Christ is the end of the law for righteousness to everyone who believes."*   (Romans 10:4)

We cannot obtain righteousness before God through the law but only through Jesus Christ who has paid the full penalty of death for each person who is under the law. The law still remains, but Jesus Christ has fulfilled the righteousness of the law.

However, Jesus Christ also fulfilled the law in another sense. He took upon Himself all of our sins and paid the final price of the law, namely death:

> *"For I delivered to you first of all that which I also received: that Christ died for our sins according to the Scriptures ..."*
>   (1 Corinthians 15:3)

Peter makes the same point:

> *" 'Who committed no sin,*
> *Nor was deceit found in His mouth';*
>
> *who, when He was reviled, did not revile in return; when He suffered, He did not threaten, but committed Himself to Him who judges righteously; who Himself bore our sins in His own body on the tree, that we, having died to sins, might live for righteousness – by whose stripes you were healed."*
>   (1 Peter 2:22–24)

Because He was sinless, Jesus Christ was the only person who fulfilled the law perfectly.

Through the law it was prophesied that Jesus would come

Moses had prophesied that God would raise up a prophet, Jesus:

> *"And the LORD said to me: ' ... I will raise up for them a Prophet like you from among their brethren, and will put My words in*

*His mouth, and He shall speak to them all that I command Him.
And it shall be that whoever will not hear My words, which He
speaks in My name, I will require it of him.'"*

(Deuteronomy 18:17, 18–19)

Peter quotes these words in Acts 3:22–26. In John's Gospel we
read:

*"Philip found Nathanael and said to him, 'We have found Him
of whom Moses in the law, and also the prophets, wrote – Jesus
of Nazareth, the son of Joseph.'"*　　　　　　　　(John 1:45)

After His death and resurrection Jesus said to His disciples:

*"These are the words which I spoke to you while I was still with
you, that all things must be fulfilled which were written in the
Law of Moses and the Prophets and the Psalms concerning Me."*

(Luke 24:44)

Jesus Christ has fulfilled the law. He was the one who Moses
prophesied would come as Messiah.

By fulfilling His sacrificial role as the Lamb of God and paying
the penalty for all sin, He gave us righteousness. He Himself led
a sinless life.

In these ways, Jesus Christ fulfilled the law. As we turn to Him
and ask Him to become our Lord and Savior, we can receive the
righteousness of God:

*"For He made Him who knew no sin to be sin for us, that we
might become the righteousness of God in Him."*

(2 Corinthians 5:21)

Summary

1. The law was the tutor to bring people to Christ.

2. The law brought a knowledge of sin.

3. The purpose of the law was to show human beings that
   they could not be made righteous by their own efforts.

4. The law foreshadowed Jesus as the Lamb of God.

5. Jesus Christ fulfilled the law.

6. Jesus paid the penalty for sin.

7. Moses prophesied that Jesus would come.

Chapter 10

Receiving God's Peace

We are given right standing with God

In his letter to the Romans, Paul teaches that the righteousness of the law is to be fulfilled in us who are followers of Jesus Christ:

> "For what the law could not do in that it was weak through the flesh, God did by sending His own Son in the likeness of sinful flesh, on account of sin: He condemned sin in the flesh, that the righteous requirement of the law might be fulfilled in us who do not walk according to the flesh but according to the Spirit."
>
> (Romans 8:3–4)

The righteousness of the law is intended to give us right standing and peace with God. As we have already seen, this is accomplished through faith in Jesus Christ and not by following the law. Because we are unable to keep the commandments of the law in full, God used a different method to save us. He destroyed sin's control over us by allowing Jesus Christ to die as a sacrifice for our sins. In response to a question from a lawyer who was tempting him, Jesus Christ summed up the righteousness of the law itself:

> "Then one of them, a lawyer, asked Him a question, testing Him, and saying, 'Teacher, which is the great commandment in the law?' Jesus said to him, 'You shall love the LORD your God with all your heart, with all your soul, and with all your mind.' This is the first and greatest commandment. And the second is like it: 'You shall love your neighbor as yourself.' On these two commandments hang all the Law and the Prophets.' "
>
> (Matthew 22:35–40)

This, in effect, is a summary of the law of Moses. The two great commandments on which hang all the law and the prophets are that we are to love the Lord our God with all our heart, with all our soul and with all our mind and, secondly, we are to love our neighbor as ourselves. Everything pales into insignificance compared with these two commandments. If we truly love the Lord our God with all our heart, soul and mind, then we will be submitting to Him, and His Son Jesus Christ, and doing the things which God has asked us to do as followers of Jesus Christ.

Paul points out the purpose of the commandment as being love:

> *"Now the purpose of the commandment is love from a pure heart, from a good conscience, and from sincere faith ... "*
>
> (1 Timothy 1:5)

This is to be from a pure heart, a good conscience and from sincere faith.

Love is the fulfillment of the law

Paul sums up this aspect of love as the fulfilling of the law in the following scripture:

> *"Owe no one anything except to love one another, for he who loves another has fulfilled the law. For the commandments, 'You shall not commit adultery,' 'You shall not murder,' 'You shall not steal,' 'You shall not bear false witness,' 'You shall not covet,' and if there is any other commandment, are all summed up in this saying, namely, 'You shall love your neighbor as yourself.' Love does no harm to a neighbor; therefore love is the fulfillment of the law."*
>
> (Romans 13:8–10)

James describes this law of love as the royal law:

> *"If you really fulfil the royal law according to the Scripture, 'You shall love your neighbor as yourself,' you do well ... "*
>
> (James 2:8)

Thus, love is the fulfillment of the law.

Jesus Christ has fulfilled the true righteousness of the law

Through faith in Jesus Christ and obedience to Him, we have right standing with God. As a result of this faith in Christ, we should love God with all our heart, soul, mind and strength, we should love our neighbor as ourselves, and we should love one another as Jesus Christ has loved us.

In both the New and Old Testaments, true righteousness is the same, i.e. love for God and love for one another. In the Old Testament this was imposed by a system from outside, whereas in the new covenant we are changed from the inside out by the grace of God.

Our heart attitude is changed by His grace, not by a law of commandments. In the new covenant, Jesus Christ comes and lives within us and by His Holy Spirit we are able to love God and love one another as He loved us. As we truly crucify our old nature daily and seek to follow Jesus Christ, then the love of God grows in our heart.

This was not possible under the law because the Holy Spirit had not been sent to the individual believer, giving that person Holy Spirit power to withstand sin. Under the old covenant a system of ordinances was imposed.

Under the new covenant, as we are born again of the Spirit of God, our life is totally changed. Our old carnal nature has been crucified at the cross of Jesus Christ.

Under the new covenant, the old stony heart is replaced by a heart of flesh. This is in accordance with the promise of God in Ezekiel:

> *"Then I will give them one heart, and I will put a new spirit within them, and take the stony heart out of their flesh, and give them a heart of flesh ... "*   (Ezekiel 11:19)

We are given a new heart and a new spirit. This affects our total attitude and conduct, as the following scripture confirms:

> *"For what the law could not do in that it was weak through the flesh, God did by sending His own Son in the likeness of sinful flesh, on account of sin: He condemned sin in the flesh, that the righteous requirement of the law might be fulfilled in us who do not walk according to the flesh but according to the Spirit."*
> (Romans 8:3–4)

The born-again believer, therefore, is able to fulfill the righteous requirement of the law because he or she will be walking now, not in accordance with the demands of the flesh, but in accordance with the Holy Spirit. As we walk in that love of

God in our relationships with others, we are fulfilling the royal law and thus the righteousness of the law.

Shall we therefore sin?

There remains one very important point, which Paul raises in his letter to the Romans:

> *"What shall we say then? Shall we continue in sin that grace may abound? Certainly not! How shall we who died to sin live any longer in it? Or do you not know that as many of us as were baptized into Christ Jesus were baptized into His death? Therefore we were buried with Him through baptism into death, that just as Christ was raised from the dead by the glory of the Father, even so we also should walk in newness of life."*
> (Romans 6:1–4)

When we come to Jesus Christ and share His death and resurrection, then our old nature should be crucified with Him.

> *"knowing this, that our old man was crucified with Him, that the body of sin might be done away with, that we should no longer be slaves of sin. For he who has died has been freed from sin."* (Romans 6:6–7)

God calls us to holiness

The fact that we have been made righteous with Jesus Christ does not give us the right to sin. God calls us to holiness:

> *"but as He who called you is holy, you also be holy in all your conduct, because it is written, 'Be holy, for I am holy.' And if you call on the Father, who without partiality judges according to each one's work, conduct yourselves throughout the time of your stay here in fear ..."* (1 Peter 1:15–17)

We have been redeemed by the precious blood of Jesus Christ

Since we have been redeemed with the precious blood of Jesus Christ, we should follow His example and avoid all deliberate sin:

> "knowing that you were not redeemed with corruptible things, like silver or gold, from your aimless conduct received by tradition from your fathers, but with the precious blood of Christ, as of a lamb without blemish and without spot."
>
> (1 Peter 1:18–19)

In addition, as we have already seen, we should do good works.

Summary

1. The righteousness of the law is fulfilled through Jesus Christ.

2. Jesus Christ gave us a new commandment that we are to love one another.

3. Love is the fulfillment of the law.

4. The true righteousness of the law is fulfilled in us as we love God and love our neighbor as ourselves.

5. Now that we are born again, we should be walking not in accordance with the demands of the flesh but in accordance with the leading of the Holy Spirit. We now have the power of the Holy Spirit and His guidance to help us in carrying out these commandments.

6. Shall we therefore sin? No! Jesus calls on us to follow His commandments.

7. We are called to holiness.

8. We have been redeemed by the precious blood of Jesus Christ.

Chapter 11

The Doctrine of Baptisms

Meaning of the word "baptism"

Dr Strong's *Exhaustive Concordance of the Bible* gives the following clear definition of the word *bapto* from which the word *baptizo* originates: "The word *bapto* means, 'To cover wholly with fluid,' that is 'to dip.' " In *Vine's Expository Dictionary of Old and New Testament Words*, the meaning of *baptizo* is given as "to dip:" it was used by the Greeks to signify the dyeing of a garment or the drawing of water by dipping one vessel into another.

Any reasonable study of this word will convince us that baptism means "immersion." It is noteworthy that this scripture refers to baptisms in the plural.

However, in Ephesians we are told:

> *"There is one body and one Spirit, just as you were called in one hope of your calling; one Lord, one faith, one baptism . . ."*
>
> (Ephesians 4:4–5)

In order to understand this particular scripture, we need to examine its context. Verse 4 refers to one body, one Spirit and one hope of our calling. There is only one body of Christ, there is only one Holy Spirit, and there is only one hope of our calling, namely Jesus Christ. There is only one Lord, that is Jesus, and there is only one true faith, and that is faith in Jesus Christ. In order to belong to the true body of believers in Jesus Christ, and to know the only true Lord and Savior Jesus Christ and the only God and Father of all, there is only one baptism. We are not baptized into a church, we are baptized into Jesus Christ.

Paul's letter to the Romans refers to this:

> *"Or do you not know that as many of us as were baptized into*
> *Christ Jesus were baptized into His death?"*   (Romans 6:3)

The example of Jesus

By being baptized Himself Jesus Christ set us a clear example.
He spoke of baptism as *"the fitting way for us to fulfill all*
righteousness" (Matthew 3:15). John baptized Him in the River
Jordan.

> *"When He had been baptized, Jesus came up immediately from*
> *the water; and behold, the heavens were opened to Him, and He*
> *saw the Spirit of God descending like a dove and alighting upon*
> *Him."*   (Matthew 3:16)

Scripture refers to several other forms of baptism:

1. Baptism of repentance

> *" 'The voice of one crying in the wilderness:*
> *"Prepare the way of the LORD;*
> *Make His paths straight." '*

> *John came baptizing in the wilderness and preaching a baptism*
> *of repentance for the remission of sins. Then all the land of*
> *Judea, and those from Jerusalem, went out to him and were all*
> *baptized by him in the Jordan River, confessing their sins."*
>   (Mark 1:3–5)

John makes it clear that the condition of the water baptism he
was preaching was that repentance should take place first. He
was preaching a baptism of repentance for the remission of sins.
As part of this baptism, people confessed their sins:

> *"Then Jerusalem, all Judea, and all the region around the Jordan*
> *went out to him and were baptized by him in the Jordan,*
> *confessing their sins."*   (Matthew 3:5–6)

However, when He saw the Pharisees and Sadducees coming to
his baptism, he said to them:

> *"Brood of vipers! Who has warned you to flee from the wrath to*
> *come. Therefore, bear fruits worthy of repentance."*
>   (Matthew 3:7–8)

Thus, it is clear that John expected evidence of repentance and confession of sins before he baptized anybody in water.

2. Baptism of suffering

Jesus Christ referred to this in Luke 12:50:

> *"But I have a baptism to be baptized with, and how distressed I am till it is accomplished!"*

He was, of course, referring to His suffering which was to take place on the cross. When James and John, the sons of Zebedee, came to Him asking Him to grant that they might sit by His side in His glory, one on His right hand and the other on His left, Jesus said to them:

> *"You do not know what you ask. Are you able to drink the cup that I drink, and be baptized with the baptism that I am baptized with?"* (Mark 10:38)

Although they said they could be baptized with this baptism, at that stage they did not understand the terrible suffering that Jesus would undergo.

3. Baptism with the Holy Spirit

This will be discussed more fully in a later chapter.

4. Baptism into Christ

The purpose of baptism into Jesus Christ is to fulfill all righteousness. This is referred to in Matthew 3:15:

> *"But Jesus answered and said to him, 'Permit it to be so now, for thus it is fitting for us to fulfill all righteousness.' Then he allowed Him."*

There is a difference between this baptism and the baptism given by John the Baptist. Jesus Christ did not need to get water baptized in order to evidence the fact that He was without sin.
  We are told in Hebrews 4:15:

> *"For we do not have a High Priest who cannot sympathize with our weaknesses, but was in all points tempted as we are, yet without sin."*

Likewise, Peter tells us:

> *"For to this you were called, because Christ also suffered for us,*
> *leaving us an example, that you should follow His steps:*
>
> > *'Who committed no sin,*
> > *Nor was deceit found in His mouth.'"*   (1 Peter 2:21–22)

When Jesus said it was fitting for us to fulfill all righteousness in this manner, He meant that He was giving us an example of how we should follow God and obey Him. By allowing Himself to be immersed in water, He was showing us what should happen in our own lives. After we have repented from sin and turned to Jesus Christ as our Lord and Savior, then we can identify with Him. He showed us how to fulfill all righteousness, by demonstrating the new state of heart and mind which comes as a result of undergoing the waters of baptism. A change has taken place in our life; we are identifying with the holiness of the Lord by turning from sin and following Him.

Just as He was obedient in fulfilling His Father's will, demonstrating His desire to fulfill that will by undergoing the waters of baptism, so, indeed, we should be prepared to undergo the waters of baptism after our conversion in order to indicate that we too are following in the footsteps of Jesus Christ.

We are not merely confirming that we have repented and turned from our sins as in John's baptism, but rather we are going further: namely, we are identifying with the death and resurrection of Jesus Christ. We are being baptized into death so that we can walk in the likeness of His resurrection. Our old nature has been crucified and we have been set free from sin. This is what our baptism should evidence.

> *"Or do you not know that as many of us as were baptized into*
> *Christ Jesus were baptized into His death? Therefore we were*
> *buried with Him through baptism into death, that just as Christ*
> *was raised from the dead by the glory of the Father, even so we*
> *also should walk in newness of life. For if we have been united*
> *together in the likeness of His death, certainly we also shall be in*
> *the likeness of His resurrection, knowing this, that our old man*
> *was crucified with Him, that the body of sin might be done away*
> *with, that we should no longer be slaves of sin. For he who has*
> *died has been freed from sin."*   (Romans 6:3–7)

Now that our old nature has died to sin we should not let that sin reign any longer in us, nor should we allow our bodies to be used for sinful purposes, but rather for the purposes of God.

> *"Likewise you also, reckon yourselves to be dead indeed to sin, but alive to God in Christ Jesus our Lord. Therefore do not let sin reign in your mortal body, that you should obey it in its lusts. And do not present your members as instruments of unrighteousness to sin, but present yourselves to God as being alive from the dead, and your members as instruments of righteousness to God. For sin shall not have dominion over you, for you are not under law but under grace."* (Romans 6:11–14)

We now become slaves of God and receive the gift of eternal life:

> *"But now having been set free from sin, and having become slaves of God, you have your fruit to holiness, and the end, everlasting life. For the wages of sin is death, but the gift of God is eternal life in Christ Jesus our Lord."* (Romans 6:22–23)

Summary

1. Baptism means "to cover wholly with fluid," that is "to dip."
2. Jesus was baptized by John in the River Jordan, saying, *"Thus it is fitting to fulfill all righteousness."*
3. John baptized with the baptism of repentance.
4. Jesus referred to the baptism of suffering which He was to undergo at the cross.
5. Another form of baptism is baptism with the Holy Spirit.
6. As we are baptized into Christ through water baptism, we identify with the death and resurrection of the Lord by turning from sin and entering into a new life in Jesus Christ.

Chapter 12

Requirements for Water Baptism

There are several steps necessary before scriptural baptism can take place:

1. Repentance

On the Day of Pentecost, after the crowd had heard Peter preach, they asked, *"Men and brethren, what shall we do?"* This is what he answered:

> *"Repent, and let every one of you be baptized in the name of Jesus Christ for the remission of sins; and you shall receive the gift of the Holy Spirit."* (Acts 2:38)

Clearly, repentance is a prior condition to baptism. Obviously, in order to repent, one must be of sufficient understanding to know that one is accountable for one's actions and, accordingly, must have reached the age of understanding.

2. Belief

In commanding His disciples to go into all the world and preach the gospel, Jesus Christ said:

> *"He who believes and is baptized will be saved; but he who does not believe will be condemned."* (Mark 16:16)

Thus, belief is required.

We find this confirmed in Acts 8, when Philip met the eunuch and explained the scriptures to him concerning Jesus Christ. When the eunuch understood that he needed to be baptized, he said: *"See, here is water. What hinders me from being baptized?"*

> *"Then Philip said, 'If you believe with all your heart, you may.' And he answered and said, 'I believe that Jesus Christ is the Son of God.'"* (Acts 8:37)

Belief is clearly a condition of water baptism.

This is in accordance with the preaching of Jesus Christ from the very beginning of His ministry:

> *"Now after John was put in prison, Jesus came to Galilee, preaching the gospel of the kingdom of God, and saying, 'The time is fulfilled, and the kingdom of God is at hand. Repent, and believe in the gospel.'"* (Mark 1:14–15)

3. A good conscience toward God

This is the third condition of water baptism.

In chapter 3 of his first epistle, Peter compares the saving of Noah and the ark with Christian baptism. The saving of Noah through water is a type of water baptism, but Peter makes it clear that water baptism is not just the removal of dirt from our flesh, but rather the answer of a good conscience toward God:

> *"There is also an antitype which now saves us – baptism (not the removal of the filth of the flesh, but the answer of a good conscience toward God), through the resurrection of Jesus Christ ..."* (1 Peter 3:21)

Water baptism is not the outward cleansing of the body, but rather signifies that there has been a total change of heart within us.

Infant baptism

Each of us must be guided by the dictates of Scripture and, of course, our own conscience. It is difficult to accept infant baptism on the basis of Scripture because it is difficult to justify it through Scripture. The reasons for this have already been clearly given, namely the need for repentance, belief and a good conscience.

Sometimes two scriptures are quoted in support of infant baptism. The first refers to the house of Cornelius in Acts 10.

Peter had been called by the Holy Spirit to the house of Cornelius to witness to this Gentile man and his household. It is clear that Cornelius and his whole household feared God:

> *"a devout man and one who feared God with all his household, who gave alms generously to the people, and prayed to God always."*   (Acts 10:2)

When Peter arrived he announced:

> *"So I sent to you immediately, and you have done well to come. Now therefore, we are all present before God, to hear all the things commanded you by God."*   (Acts 10:33)

It is clear that those present had the ability to hear and understand the things which Peter would say.

As we look further on in Scripture, we find these words:

> *"While Peter was still speaking these words, the Holy Spirit fell upon all those who heard the word."*   (Acts 10:44)

Here, clearly, the Holy Spirit fell upon all who heard the word. Then an amazing thing happened:

> *"For they heard them speak with tongues and magnify God ... "*
>   (Acts 10:46)

Everybody present was speaking in tongues and magnifying God. This could hardly apply to infants.

Cornelius sees an angel

Later, when he was recounting his experience, Peter told how Cornelius had sent for him, saying he had seen an angel standing in his house:

> *"And he told us how he had seen an angel standing in his house, who said to him, 'Send men to Joppa, and call for Simon whose surname is Peter, who will tell you words by which you and all your household will be saved.'"*   (Acts 11:13–14)

Thus, it would seem clear that all of those present were capable of repenting, believing and having a good conscience toward God.

The woman named Lydia

The second instance refers to a certain woman named Lydia. Scripture tells us she was a seller of purple from the city of Thyatira, who worshipped God. After the Lord opened her understanding to heed the words spoken by Paul we read:

> *"And when she and her household were baptized, she begged us, saying, 'If you have judged me to be faithful to the Lord, come to my house and stay.' So she persuaded us."*   (Acts 16:15)

No conclusion can be drawn from this Scripture in favor of or against infant baptism. However, the conditions that we have already referred to relative to baptism would indicate no infant baptism took place there.

Paul and Silas in jail

The third instance refers to the experience of Paul and Silas while they were in jail at Philippi. At midnight they were praying and singing hymns to God when an earthquake took place. The keeper of the prison, fearing that all the prisoners had escaped, was about to kill himself when Paul and Silas called out to reassure him. He brought them out of their prison cell and said: *"Sirs, what must I do to be saved?"* (Acts 16:30)

> *"So they said, 'Believe on the Lord Jesus Christ, and you will be saved, you and your household.' Then they spoke the word of the Lord to him and to all who were in his house. And he took them the same hour of the night and washed their stripes. And immediately he and all his family were baptized. Now when he had brought them into his house, he set food before them; and he rejoiced, having believed in God with all his household."*
>
> (Acts 16:31–34)

It is clear from reading these scriptures that, after Paul and Silas had spoken the word of the Lord to him and all who were in his house (verse 32), then he and all his family were baptized (verse 33), having believed in God with all his household (verse 34).

Obviously, since his whole household believed, they must have been of an age of understanding to do so.

What about infants?

In the Old Testament there is a clear indication that under a certain age persons were not accountable for their sins.

When the Lord told Moses to spy out the land of Canaan which He was giving to the children of Israel, He instructed him to select a man from each of the twelve tribes. After these men had spied out the land and come back with a good report, two of them, Caleb and Joshua, wanted to go into the Promised Land immediately, but the other ten were fearful and persuaded the people not to do so. Then all the people murmured against Moses and Aaron:

> *"And all the children of Israel complained against Moses and Aaron, and the whole congregation said to them, 'If only we had died in the land of Egypt! Or if only we had died in this wilderness! Why has the LORD brought us to this land to fall by the sword, that our wives and children should become victims? Would it not be better for us to return to Egypt?' So they said to one another, 'Let us select a leader and return to Egypt.'"*
>
> (Numbers 14:2–4)

At this God became extremely angry:

> *"How long shall I bear with this evil congregation who complain against Me? I have heard the complaints which the children of Israel make against Me ... Say to them, 'As I live,' says the LORD, 'just as you have spoken in My hearing, so I will do to you: The carcasses of you who have complained against Me shall fall in this wilderness, all of you who were numbered according to your entire number, from twenty years old and above. Except for Caleb the son of Jephunneh and Joshua the son of Nun, you shall by no means enter the land which I swore I would make you dwell in.'"*
>
> (Numbers 14:27–30)

God makes an exception for the little ones

Apart from Caleb and Joshua, God made a further exception:

> *"But your little ones, whom you said would be victims, I will bring in, and they shall know the land which you have despised."*
>
> (Numbers 14:31)

In other words, He excluded the little ones from this judgment because they had obviously not reached the age of understanding.

This is further confirmed in Deuteronomy 1:

> *"Moreover your little ones and your children, who you say will be victims, who today have no knowledge of good and evil, they shall go in there; to them I will give it, and they shall possess it."*
> (Deuteronomy 1:39)

Here we see a clear statement that these children had no knowledge of good or evil and, therefore, they were exempted from God's judgment.

The whole generation of those who had acted disobediently was destroyed:

> *"And the time we took to come from Kadesh Barnea until we crossed over the Valley of the Zered was thirty-eight years, until all the generation of the men of war was consumed from the midst of the camp, just as the LORD had sworn to them."*
> (Deuteronomy 2:14)

The age of accountability

It will also be noted that those who were numbered were twenty years old and above. Because those under twenty years did survive, it is clear that God only held those accountable who were over that age.

In the new covenant it would also seem that there is a difference between children and adults. Jesus said about the children:

> *"Take heed that you do not despise one of these little ones, for I say to you that in heaven their angels always see the face of My Father who is in heaven."*   (Matthew 18:10)

Here we have a clear indication from Jesus that the angels of children always see the face of God the Father. Little children are not to be despised because in heaven their angels are always looking at the face of the Father. This would indicate that the protection of God's angels is around children while they are of a young age.

In the Old Testament, God spoke to Israel as a nation. In the New Testament, because Jesus Christ came and died for individual believers, then He speaks to each person personally as the Holy Spirit draws them. As we reach the age of understanding, we are called upon to respond to the gospel of Jesus Christ.

This age of understanding may differ from one person to another.

Once, however, we do have the call of God upon our hearts and are old enough to understand the gospel of Jesus Christ, then God expects us to respond. After that response water baptism should take place. A person reaches the age of understanding when he or she comes to know the meaning of sin and the need for repentance and belief in God. This is the age at which we should listen to God and repent, after which water baptism can take place.

It is appropriate to dedicate infants to the Lord in the same way that Jesus Christ was taken to the temple and dedicated:

> *"Now when the days of her purification according to the law of Moses were completed, they brought Him to Jerusalem to present Him to the Lord ... "*   (Luke 2:22)

Having been dedicated to the Lord, they should be brought up in the nurture and admonition of the Lord so that when they attain the age of understanding, they can truly repent and undergo the waters of baptism.

The age of accountability obviously depends on the age of understanding. For one person the age of understanding may be five or six years of age, for another it may be eight years of age. God knows each individual heart.

Therefore, it is clear that the age of understanding is the time when we can come to know the meaning of sin, the need for repentance and belief in God. This is the age at which we should listen to God, and, after true repentance has taken place, we can be baptized in water.

Summary

1. Repentance is a prior condition to baptism in water.

2. Belief is required.

3. It is necessary to have a good conscience toward God.

4. In the Old Testament, God did not hold persons account-able until they reached the age of understanding. At the time of Moses, this was twenty years of age.

5. In the Old Testament, God dealt with His people, Israel, as a nation.

6. In the New Testament, God deals with us as individuals. Jesus Christ has died for each one of us individually and we need to respond to the gospel accordingly.

7. When we reach the age of understanding, namely the age at which we can understand sin, the need for repentance and belief in God, then this will be the age at which God will hold us accountable. At this point we should repent, turn to God and be baptized in water.

8. Jesus Christ was taken as an infant to the temple and dedicated to the Lord.

9. Children should be dedicated to the Lord and brought up in the nurture and admonition of the Lord.

Chapter 13

The Effects of Water Baptism

Water baptism cuts us off from our previous life. I have found that when I have preached the gospel in India, many would want to know Jesus the great prophet, but not Jesus the Messiah. Once we preach Jesus as the Messiah, namely the only way, the only truth and the only life, then we are clearly distinguishing the Jesus of the Bible from a Jesus whom the Hindus would name as one of their gods.

It is comparatively easy to encourage people in India to turn to Jesus Christ as Lord and Savior. However, it is a different matter when we ask them to be baptized in water. Most of them know that if they do so, then they will be cut off from their family, who no longer will have anything to do with them. They become a pariah.

This not only applies in India, but many other countries. Most religions understand the meaning of baptism, namely that it is a change of direction from a previous way of living.

However, baptism into Jesus Christ is something even greater than this. Water baptism signifies:

Dying to sin

> "What shall we say then? Shall we continue in sin that grace may abound? Certainly not! How shall we who died to sin live any longer in it?" (Romans 6:1–2)

Once we have been baptized into Jesus Christ, we should no longer live a life of deliberate sin.

Baptism into His death

Water baptism into Jesus Christ means we are baptized into His death:

> *"Or do you not know that as many of us as were baptized into Christ Jesus were baptized into His death?"* (Romans 6:3)

In other words, we identify with Jesus Christ in His death and resurrection. Just as He went into Sheol and then rose out of it into resurrection life, so we die to our old life and enter into a new life in Jesus Christ.

When Bill Subritzky was born again, then the old Bill Subritzky died. When we are born again, then our old self should die and a new person in Jesus Christ should replace it.

We should then walk in newness of life:

> *"Therefore we were buried with Him through baptism into death, that just as Christ was raised from the dead by the glory of the Father, even so we also should walk in newness of life."*
> (Romans 6:4)

Resurrection

Just as we have identified with Jesus Christ in His death, so we should identify with Him in resurrection:

> *"For if we have been united together in the likeness of His death, certainly we also shall be in the likeness of His resurrection ... "*
> (Romans 6:5)

Old nature crucified daily

Now that we have been baptized, we agree that our old nature has been crucified so that our sinful nature should be done away with. At the Fall, the whole of humankind fell. We were condemned to a spiritual death. When we come to Jesus Christ and are baptized into Him, we enter into spiritual life.

> *"knowing this, that our old man was crucified with Him, that the body of sin might be done away with, that we should no longer be slaves of sin."* (Romans 6:6)

This is why Paul said he died daily.

> *"I affirm, by the boasting in you which I have in Christ Jesus our Lord, I die daily."* (1 Corinthians 15:31)

Every day we should crucify our old nature. Every morning when we wake up, it will seek to rise up and take us over.

It is full of "gimme this" and "gimme that." The old nature is represented by the old self. It is very fashionable today to talk about "self-actualization," "self-realization," "self-esteem," etc.

All of these 'selfs' are the old nature. They need to be killed off. We need to put the old self on the cross daily so that we can identify with Jesus Christ in every part of our life.

As we crucify the old nature, then our new nature in Christ can grow. That is when the fruit of the Holy Spirit can begin to fill our life. This fruit is love, joy, peace, long-suffering, kindness, goodness, faithfulness, gentleness and self-control (Galatians 5:22–23).

No power or dominion
When we die to our old selves, then we are freed from sin:

> *"For he who has died has been freed from sin."*   (Romans 6:7)

Sin no longer has any power or dominion over us. The power of the Holy Spirit enables us to walk with the Lord and to resist the works of the world, the flesh and the devil. We will never have that power of resistance unless we are walking in this new life.

If our father has beaten us or sexually abused us, or our mother has acted wrongly toward us, we will find it extremely difficult to forgive him or her. It is only when Jesus Christ comes into our lives and the Holy Spirit lives within us that we have this power to forgive.

The world never understands this forgiveness. We often see television programs discussing these matters. People are told, "You don't need to forgive," or "You shouldn't forgive," or "You should hate." By following such advice, the old carnal nature is fed. Our old man should be dead. It stinks. It shouldn't be fed at all.

We are only freed from sin as we walk in the Holy Spirit with Jesus Christ as our Lord and Savior and fully appropriate the work of the cross in our lives.

On the cross, Jesus Christ has delivered us from the power of sin and sickness:

> *"Surely He has borne our griefs*
> *And carried our sorrows;*
> *Yet we esteemed Him stricken,*

Smitten by God, and afflicted.
But He was wounded for our transgressions,
He was bruised for our iniquities;
The chastisement for our peace was upon Him,
And by His stripes we are healed." (Isaiah 53:4–5)

"Griefs" is more correctly translated "sicknesses" from the Greek word *cholee*, and "sorrows" should be translated "pains" (Greek *mahob*).

On the cross, Jesus Christ became an offering for sin: He carried our sins.

We need to understand that when we come to the cross of Jesus Christ in true repentance and follow Him, then all our sins have been forgiven.

This is why Jesus Christ said:

> *"If anyone desires to come after Me, let him deny himself, and take up his cross daily, and follow Me."* (Luke 9:23)

Taking up our cross daily
Yes, we should take up our cross daily and follow Jesus. This means applying the cross to every part of our life. As someone has said, the cross of Jesus Christ is where our will meets the will of God. If we do not subject our own will to the will of God, then we will never freely walk with Him.

I find that many people blame demons for what is, in effect, their old nature. They may have habits or attitudes from which they want to be set free, but, rather than being demonic in nature, the problem is often simply that they have never truly repented and decided to crucify the old nature.

It is important to remember that we cannot crucify demons or cast out the old nature. The old nature must be crucified and the demons must be cast out.

So, before we start blaming the demons for our problems, let us be sure that we have truly repented and taken up our cross daily to follow Jesus Christ. Each day we crucify our old nature so that it does not rise up and take over our attitudes, our habits and our thoughts.

Living with Him
When we identify with the death of Jesus Christ, then we have confidence that we shall live in eternal life with Him. Jesus Christ will never die again. He has died for us all and death no

longer has any dominion over Him. He died to become a sin offering for us, but now He has been resurrected from the dead and is seated at the right hand of God.

Therefore, we are told to reckon ourselves to be dead to sin, but alive to God in Christ Jesus. We should not allow sin to dominate our lives any more.

When we are born again of the Spirit of God, a spark or flame of God develops within us and we know that we have the Spirit of God.

Refusing to sin

That is why we should not let sin take over our mortal body. We should refuse to obey sin and realize we have entered into spiritual life with God. We should allow our body to be used only for purposes pleasing to God:

> *"knowing that Christ, having been raised from the dead, dies no more. Death no longer has dominion over Him. For the death that He died, He died to sin once for all; but the life that He lives, He lives to God. Likewise you also, reckon yourselves to be dead indeed to sin, but alive to God in Christ Jesus our Lord. Therefore do not let sin reign in your mortal body, that you should obey it in its lusts. And do not present your members as instruments of unrighteousness to sin, but present yourselves to God as being alive from the dead, and your members as instruments of righteousness to God. For sin shall not have dominion over you, for you are not under law but under grace."* (Romans 6:9–14)

Our own desires tempt us

James warns us that it is our own desires which lead us into temptation:

> *"But each one is tempted when he is drawn away by his own desires and enticed. Then, when desire has conceived, it gives birth to sin; and sin, when it is full-grown, brings forth death."*
> (James 1:14–15)

It is by allowing our own desires to take over and opening ourselves to sin that lust can gain a hold in our lives. That is why Jesus said:

> *"But I say to you that whoever looks at a woman to lust for her has already committed adultery with her in his heart."*
> (Matthew 5:28)

Not free to sin

Some people have suggested that because we are no longer under the law but under grace, we are free to sin. This, of course, is quite wrong. We should not seek to take advantage of the grace of God, but should seek to obey Him at all times.

If we obey sin, then we become a slave to sin, which will lead us into spiritual death.

We should become slaves of righteousness or, as the scripture says, slaves of God, so that we may bear the fruit of holiness and finally enter into everlasting life:

> *"But now having been set free from sin, and having become slaves of God, you have your fruit to holiness, and the end, everlasting life."* (Romans 6:22)

Scripture says:

> *"For the wages of sin is death, but the gift of God is eternal life in Christ Jesus our Lord."* (Romans 6:23)

Effects of true repentance

I have heard people testify that they were baptized in water on more than twenty occasions, but nothing happened to them. They carried on in their old sin.

This was because there was no real repentance in their lives. They had never been truly born again of the Spirit of God.

However, I have heard these same people say that when they did finally turn to God in true repentance, immediately their hearts were changed. When they went under the waters of baptism subsequent to their decision to follow the Lord and obey Him wholeheartedly, then their water baptism became meaningful.

It is clear from Scripture that our baptism into Christ must follow our act of repentance and truly turning to God. The act of water baptism should be an outward sign of what has already inwardly happened in our heart.

As Paul expresses it so perfectly under the anointing of the Holy Spirit:

> *"I have been crucified with Christ; it is no longer I who live, but Christ lives in me; and the life which I now live in the flesh I live by faith in the Son of God, who loved me and gave Himself for me."* (Galatians 2:20)

Summary

1. We should no longer live lives of deliberate sin.

2. In water baptism, we identify with Jesus Christ in His death and resurrection. We thus die to our old life and enter into a new life in Jesus Christ.

3. Just as we have been united together in the likeness of His death, so we shall be united together in the likeness of His resurrection.

4. In water baptism we acknowledge that our old nature has been crucified so that our sinful nature is done away with. We should crucify our old nature daily.

5. Sin no longer has any power or dominion over us.

6. We should take up our cross daily and follow Jesus.

7. We should not allow sin to dominate our lives any more.

8. We should refuse to sin.

9. We are enticed away from God by our own desires.

10. We are not free to sin because we should become slaves of righteousness so that we bear the fruit of holiness and finally enter everlasting life.

11. The effect of true repentance is that we acknowledge that we have been crucified with Christ; we do not live for ourselves but Christ lives in us. We live by faith in the Son of God who loved us and gave Himself for us.

Chapter 14

Baptism with the Holy Spirit

Another doctrine of baptisms is known as the baptism with the Holy Spirit. Through this baptism, we receive power to witness.

On the Sunday night of His resurrection, when Jesus Christ met with ten of His disciples, He said:

> "'Peace to you! As the Father has sent Me, I also send you.' And when He had said this, He breathed on them, and said to them, 'Receive the Holy Spirit.'" (John 20:21–22)

Among those disciples was Peter.

It is clear from this scripture that, as Jesus Christ breathed on His disciples, they received the Holy Spirit. Similarly, when we come to Jesus Christ in true repentance and submit to Him as Lord and Savior, the Holy Spirit is breathed on us and we receive Him.

When Jesus Christ breathed on His disciples in this manner, they became life-giving spirits. In Genesis 2:7, we read:

> "And the LORD God formed man of the dust of the ground, and breathed into his nostrils the breath of life; and man became a life-giving being." (Genesis 2:7)

Then man became a living soul. Now he can become a life-giving being by receiving the Holy Spirit.

Despite the fact that these ten disciples had already received the Holy Spirit, these words appear in Luke's Gospel:

> "Behold, I send the Promise of My Father upon you; but tarry in the city of Jerusalem until you are endued with power from on high." (Luke 24:49)

Jesus Christ is now referring to the Promise of His Father. What is that promise?

Jesus baptizes with the Holy Spirit

In each of the Gospels, we find that Jesus Christ is described as Baptizer in the Holy Spirit:

> *"I indeed baptize you with water unto repentance, but He who is coming after me is mightier than I, whose sandals I am not worthy to carry. He will baptize you with the Holy Spirit and fire."*   (Matthew 3:11)

> *"I indeed baptized you with water, but He will baptize you with the Holy Spirit."*   (Mark 1:8)

> *"John answered, saying to all, 'I indeed baptize you with water; but One mightier than I is coming, whose sandal strap I am not worthy to loose. He will baptize you with the Holy Spirit and fire.'"*   (Luke 3:16)

> *"I did not know Him, but He who sent me to baptize with water said to me, 'Upon whom you see the Spirit descending, and remaining on Him, this is He who baptizes with the Holy Spirit.'"*   (John 1:33)

We have previously seen that to baptize means to "immerse" or to "cover or fill thoroughly."

It is significant that Scripture describes Jesus as the person who covers, fills or immerses us in the Holy Spirit.

To grasp the full meaning of this aspect of Holy Spirit baptism, we need to turn to Acts 1:4–5:

> *"And being assembled together with them, He commanded them not to depart from Jerusalem, but to wait for the Promise of the Father, 'which,' He said, 'you have heard from Me; for John truly baptized with water, but you shall be baptized with the Holy Spirit not many days from now.'"*

Thus Jesus Christ told His disciples not to leave Jerusalem, but to wait for the Promise of the Father, which is the same promise we read about in Luke 24:49.

He promised that they would be baptized with the Holy Spirit. He did not say they would be baptized with water, but with the Holy Spirit.

Obedience of the disciples

The disciples were obedient. This is the great hallmark of the early Church, namely obedience to Jesus Christ.

Too often today, we want to run off and do our own thing. Let us remember that the ten disciples present on the Sunday night of the resurrection of Jesus Christ, had already received the Holy Spirit. They did not say, "We have enough," or "There is no more," or "There is no other experience." They simply obeyed the Lord. That is what God calls upon us to do today. If we did this, and our churches really obeyed God in this respect and sought this experience, then how totally changed our churches would be!

Jesus refers further to this experience in Acts 1:8:

> *"But you shall receive power when the Holy Spirit has come upon you; and you shall be witnesses to Me in Jerusalem, and in all Judea and Samaria, and to the end of the earth."*

Jesus taken up and received by a cloud

After Jesus had spoken these words, He was taken up and *"a cloud received Him out of their sight."*

The last words that Jesus Christ said to His disciples on this earth were that they would receive power when the Holy Spirit came upon them and they would be witnesses in Jerusalem, Judea, Samaria and to the ends of the earth.

The occasion was a momentous one. This would be the last time that Jesus would be seen alive walking this earth before His second coming. The importance of these last words spoken by Him on this earth cannot be over-emphasized.

We find that the disciples were obedient. They had walked with Jesus Christ for forty days after His resurrection and had eaten with Him. During this time, He had spoken of things pertaining to the kingdom of God.

The Day of Pentecost

Now they waited a further ten days, as the Day of Pentecost approached. On the day of that great feast, a wonderful experience happened:

*"When the Day of Pentecost had fully come, they were all with
one accord in one place. And suddenly there came a sound from
heaven, as of a rushing mighty wind, and it filled the whole
house where they were sitting. Then there appeared to them
divided tongues, as of fire, and one sat upon each of them. And
they were all filled with the Holy Spirit and began to speak with
other tongues, as the Spirit gave them utterance."* (Acts 2:1–4)

Thus, Peter and the other disciples who were present on the
Sunday night of the resurrection of Jesus Christ, were now all
filled with the Holy Spirit and began to speak with other
tongues as the Holy Spirit gave them the ability.

These were men who had already received the Holy Spirit, but
now they were all filled with the Holy Spirit. This is the baptism
with the Holy Spirit, with Jesus Christ as the Baptizer.

The response of the crowd

As frequently happens when the world does not understand, it
mocks the Christian experience.

At that time there were Jews from fifteen nations living
in Jerusalem. When they heard the 120 disciples speaking in
tongues, they were amazed. They could hear the disciples
speaking in their own languages about the wonderful works of
God.

Some asked what could this mean, but others said, *"They are
full of new wine,"* implying that they were drunk.

Peter's first sermon

As a result of this experience, Peter was now fully empowered by
the Holy Spirit. No longer was he the frightened disciple who
had denied Jesus Christ three times. He was now under the full
anointing of God and he began to preach to the assembled
crowd. He denied that the disciples were drunk as it was still
only 9 o'clock in the morning.

However, he reminded the people that this is what the
prophet Joel had prophesied:

*'"And it shall come to pass in the last days, says God,
That I will pour out of My Spirit on all flesh;
Your sons and your daughters shall prophesy,
Your young men shall see visions,*

Your old men shall dream dreams.
And on My menservants and on My maidservants
I will pour out My Spirit in those days;
And they shall prophesy.' "   (Acts 2:17–18)

He then told them that Jesus Christ was no longer in the grave with His body subject to corruption, but rather was seated at the right hand of God. David had prophesied these events, including the fact that God would raise up, from the descendants of David, Jesus Christ to sit on His throne.

> *"he, foreseeing this, spoke concerning the resurrection of the Christ, that His soul was not left in Hades, nor did His flesh see corruption. This Jesus God has raised up, of which we are all witnesses. Therefore being exalted to the right hand of God, and having received from the Father the promise of the Holy Spirit, He poured out this which you now see and hear."*
>   (Acts 2:31–33)

From this it can be seen that Jesus Christ is now seated at the right hand of God and, having received from God the Father the promise of the Holy Spirit, has now poured it out.

With great boldness Peter challenged his hearers:

> *"Repent, and let every one of you be baptized in the name of Jesus Christ for the remission of sins; and you shall receive the gift of the Holy Spirit. For the promise is to you and to your children, and to all who are afar off, as many as the Lord our God will call."*   (Acts 2:38–39)

We read that three thousand people were saved that day and fear came upon every person and many wonders and signs were done through the apostles.

We too can be empowered in exactly the same way as we wait upon the Lord and allow Jesus Christ to baptize us with the Holy Spirit.

Summary

1. On the Sunday night of His resurrection, Jesus Christ breathed on His disciples and said, *"Receive the Holy Spirit."* We contrast this with the statement in Genesis 2:7, when God formed man out of the dust of the ground and breathed into his nostrils the breath of life, and man became a living being.

2. In Genesis we read that man became a living soul. After the resurrection of Jesus Christ we can become a life-giving spirit by receiving the Holy Spirit.

3. Jesus is the Baptizer with the Holy Spirit.

4. The obedience of the disciples to the commands of Jesus Christ led to them receiving the baptism with the Holy Spirit on the Day of Pentecost.

5. The disciples were now filled with the Holy Spirit and began to speak with other tongues as the Holy Spirit gave them the ability.

6. As is usual, the world mocks true spiritual experiences. In this case the people said, *"They are full of new wine."*

7. However, Peter, now fully empowered by the Holy Spirit, preached his first sermon.

8. He explained that Jesus Christ is seated at the right hand of God and has poured out the Promise of the Father which is what they were now seeing and hearing.

Chapter 15

Results of the Baptism with the Holy Spirit

As we have seen, on the very first day of the feast of Pentecost, three thousand people were saved. Shortly afterwards we read the story of a man who had been lame for forty years. He was healed when he met Peter and John at the Beautiful Gate of the temple. In response to the lame man's request for alms, now Peter was able to say:

"Silver and gold I do not have, but what I do have I give you: In the name of Jesus Christ of Nazareth, rise up and walk."

(Acts 3:6)

Peter took the man by the right hand and lifted him onto his feet. Immediately his feet and ankle bones received strength and he started walking, leaping and praising God.

1. Boldness in preaching

With great boldness, Peter then began to preach:

"So when Peter saw it, he responded to the people: 'Men of Israel, why do you marvel at this? Or why look so intently at us, as though by our own power or godliness we had made this man walk? The God of Abraham, Isaac, and Jacob, the God of our fathers, glorified His Servant Jesus, whom you delivered up and denied in the presence of Pilate, when he was determined to let Him go. But you denied the Holy One and the Just, and asked for a murderer to be granted to you, and killed the Prince of life, whom God raised from the dead, of which we are witnesses. And

His name, through faith in His name, has made this man strong,
whom you see and know. Yes, the faith which comes through
Him has given him this perfect soundness in the presence of you
all.'"   (Acts 3:12–16)

2. Fear disappears

Even when they were arrested and accused in front of the rulers,
elders and scribes, the disciples had no fear. Now they had the
boldness of the Holy Spirit, no longer were they wanting to run
away. We see this again in Acts 4:33:

"And with great power the apostles gave witness to the resur-
rection of the Lord Jesus. And great grace was upon them all."

3. Gifts of the Holy Spirit

Immediately they began to operate in the gifts of the Holy
Spirit. We see Peter operating in the gift of discernment of
spirits when he pointed out that Ananias had allowed Satan to
fill his heart with lies:

"But Peter said, 'Ananias, why has Satan filled your heart to lie
to the Holy Spirit and keep back part of the price of the land for
yourself?'"   (Acts 5:3)

4. Preaching

Even after they were arrested and beaten again, they would not
stop teaching and preaching Jesus as the Christ:

"And daily in the temple, and in every house, they did not cease
teaching and preaching Jesus as the Christ."   (Acts 5:42)

5. Full of faith and power

People like Stephen were full of faith and power and they did
great signs and wonders among the people.

In Acts 8 we read that Philip went down to the city of Samaria
and preached Christ to the people there. Unclean spirits, crying
with a loud voice, came out of many who were possessed, and
many who were paralysed and lame were healed. He was
anointed with great power by the Holy Spirit.

On hearing that Samaria had received the word of God, the apostles, who were at Jerusalem, sent Peter and John to them.

These people had been baptized in the name of the Lord Jesus Christ. They had believed Philip as he preached about the kingdom of God and the name of Jesus, and accordingly had been baptized in water.

Thus, these people would have received the Holy Spirit – but they had not yet been baptized with the Holy Spirit. This had to wait until the apostles arrived.

We must remember that the people of Samaria followed a mixture of religions and the Jews despised them. Although young Philip had been preaching the gospel with great power, nevertheless, God wanted the apostles, themselves, to see how His Holy Spirit was moving, even among the Samaritans.

The apostles were led by the Holy Spirit to lay hands on the people who then received the Holy Spirit.

When Simon the sorcerer saw that, through the laying on of the apostles' hands, the Holy Spirit was given to the new believers, he offered the apostles money. He said:

> *"Give me this power also, that anyone on whom I lay hands may receive the Holy Spirit."*   (Acts 8:19)

Obviously Simon saw something happening. It is fair to infer that he saw the people of Samaria speaking in tongues as the Holy Spirit came upon them.

The power of God was not confined to the Jews.

6. The Gentiles are baptized with the Holy Spirit

Peter at Cornelius's house

Peter was called to the house of Cornelius, a Gentile, where he testified about Jesus Christ (see also pp. 90–91.).

Describing himself as one of those who had eaten and drunk with Jesus after His resurrection, he told how Jesus Christ had commanded the disciples to preach to the people and testified that it was Jesus who was ordained by God to be judge of the living and the dead. He pointed out that the prophets witnessed that, through the name of Jesus, whoever believes in Him will receive forgiveness of sins.

He had barely finished speaking when we read that the Holy

Spirit fell upon all those who heard the word. Obviously these Gentiles were believing:

> *"And those of the circumcision who believed were astonished, as many as came with Peter, because the gift of the Holy Spirit had been poured out on the Gentiles also. For they heard them speak with tongues and magnify God. Then Peter answered, 'Can anyone forbid water, that these should not be baptized who have received the Holy Spirit just as we have?'"*   (Acts 10:45–47)

Here we have the situation where the Holy Spirit fell upon the people before they were baptized in water. Obviously God is sovereign. We cannot demand that He follows any particular order of doing things. He does it in His own way.

Paul at Ephesus
When Paul was involved in one of his great missionary journeys, he came to Ephesus. There he found some disciples who had not even heard that there was a Holy Spirit. They had been baptized into John's baptism.

We read what happened when He told them about Jesus:

> *"When they heard this, they were baptized in the name of the Lord Jesus. And when Paul had laid hands on them, the Holy Spirit came upon them, and they spoke with tongues and prophesied."*   (Acts 19:5–6)

7. Gift of tongues

We should not confuse this gift with the gift of a public tongue referred to in 1 Corinthians 12:10. The gift of tongues received in the baptism with the Holy Spirit enables us to pray directly to God, bypassing our natural mind.

However, the gift of a public tongue is an ability, given to specific individuals, to bring a message by their new language, which is either interpreted by that person or another. This particular gift of speaking in a public tongue is not given to everybody. Like the other gifts referred to in 1 Corinthians 12, it is distributed by the Holy Spirit as He wills.

In my experience, I have found that many people have questions about the baptism with the Holy Spirit. However, when they genuinely seek this experience and are baptized into the Holy Spirit, they have no more questions.

8. Long tarrying not necessary

Fifty years ago, many people thought that it was necessary to tarry day and night for this experience. Therefore, they waited many weeks and even months to receive it.

They had focused on the scripture in Luke 24:49, when Jesus told His disciples to "tarry" in the city of Jerusalem. Some people had "tarrying parties," waiting for the baptism with the Spirit.

However, this was not really necessary, because this specific command only applied to Jesus' first disciples whom Jesus told to wait in Jerusalem.

During the great charismatic renewal of the past twenty-five years, many have come into the baptism with the Holy Spirit simply by asking Jesus Christ to baptize them with the Holy Spirit. The fact is that God has already granted this gift through Jesus Christ: this gift of the Promise of the Father. All we have to do is to believe and receive it.

Sometimes we find that people have a real blockage in receiving this gift. Perhaps they have been taught that it is not for today or there has been an occultic background in their lives. On other occasions we find that people cannot receive because of an intellectual blockage.

When I pray for people for the baptism with the Holy Spirit, I always encourage them to renounce any fear, doubt, unbelief, blockage of mind, the occult, wrong doctrine and anything else that would prevent them from coming into this experience.

When we ask Jesus Christ to baptize anyone with the Holy Spirit, we should ensure that the person is truly repentant before God and is born again of the Holy Spirit.

Having ensured that this is so, it is good to ask Jesus Christ, as the Baptizer with the Holy Spirit, to baptize people with the Holy Spirit from the top of their head to the soles of their feet. Invariably, as people begin to open their mouth, God will give them a new language. If they are prepared to open their mouth and trust God, not allowing their natural mind to block what God is doing, they will find that they will readily come into this experience.

The Holy Spirit helps us in our weaknesses

The Holy Spirit helps us in our weaknesses. Not only does the baptism with the Holy Spirit fill us with His presence in our lives, but we now have an ability to pray to God bypassing our natural mind. Sometimes after we have prayed for a while, we cannot think of anything further to pray, but now we can allow the Holy Spirit to help us:

> *"Likewise the Spirit also helps in our weaknesses. For we do not know what we should pray for as we ought, but the Spirit Himself makes intercession for us with groanings which cannot be uttered."*   (Romans 8:26)

Casting out of demons

This power experience is a wonderful way to cast out demons. Quite frequently, as we pray in tongues, the demonic power flees in terror because it knows that we are praying to God with real power.

How to receive

I have never yet seen anybody who has earnestly sought this experience, fail to receive it. Many people have even found this experience by kneeling in their own bedroom and seeking God for it.

If you wish to, why don't you do so right now? Find a quiet place, get down on your knees, confess your sins to God and declare that Jesus Christ is your Lord and Savior. Perhaps you could say this prayer:

> "Dear Heavenly Father, I come to You in the name of Jesus Christ. I confess my sins to You now ....
> .... [*name sins*].
> I confess that Jesus Christ is my Lord and my Savior. I confess that He is the only way to God. I confess that Jesus Christ is the way, the truth and the life.
> In the name of Jesus Christ, I now renounce all fear, doubt, unbelief, blockage of mind, wrong doctrine and every involvement in the occult. I specifically renounce the following involvement in the occult ....
> ....
> I specifically renounce all unforgiveness. I honor my parents.
> I ask You, Lord Jesus, to baptize me with Your Holy Spirit, from the top of my head to the soles of my feet."

Now, if you will open your mouth and speak out, believing God will give you a new language, you will find the power of God will overflow you as Jesus baptizes you with the Holy Spirit.

Even if you do not come into the gift of tongues immediately, continue to believe that God will grant you this gift. As you continue to believe and endeavour to speak out in your new language, you will find that God will empower you and grant you this gift.

Summary

1. As soon as they received the baptism with the Holy Spirit Peter and the others began to preach with great boldness.

2. They preached without fear and with great power.

3. The early Church began to operate in the gifts of the Holy Spirit.

4. The early Church did not cease teaching and preaching Jesus as the Christ.

5. People like Stephen and Philip were full of faith and power.

6. To the astonishment of Peter, the Gentiles in the house of Cornelius were baptized with the Holy Spirit.

7. In the house of Cornelius, the Holy Spirit fell upon the people before they were baptized in water.

8. We should distinguish the gift of a public tongue referred to in 1 Corinthians 12:10 from the gift of tongues received in the baptism with the Holy Spirit.

9. With great power, Peter now exhorted the assembled throng to repent and be baptized in the name of Jesus Christ.

10. Three thousand people responded that day to the gospel of Jesus Christ.

11. It is usually not necessary to wait for long periods to receive the baptism with the Holy Spirit.

12. The Holy Spirit helps us in our weaknesses. We have an ability to pray directly to God bypassing our natural mind.

13. The baptism with the Holy Spirit increases our prayer power, especially in ministry against demons.

14. The baptism with the Holy Spirit gives us a greatly increased power to witness.

15. We can receive the baptism with the Holy Spirit in a simple act of faith and belief.

Chapter 16

The Laying On of Hands

The Old Testament

Scripture sets out three reasons for the laying on of hands:

1. to impart a gift or blessing
2. to carry the sins of others
3. to set apart for service.

1. To impart a blessing

The first reference we find to the laying on of hands in Scripture is in the book of Genesis when Israel, who was formerly named Jacob, laid hands on his grandchildren, Ephraim and Manasseh:

> *"Then Israel stretched out his right hand and laid it on Ephraim's head, who was the younger, and his left hand on Manasseh's head, guiding his hands knowingly, for Manasseh was the firstborn."* (Genesis 48:14)

Joseph had expected his father, Israel, to lay his right hand on the head of Manasseh as the first-born, but, instead, he laid his right hand on Ephraim and his left hand on Manasseh.

In this case the purpose of the laying on of hands was to impart blessing. In normal circumstances, the first-born, Manasseh, should have received the greater blessing. However, even though Israel was nearly blind, he knew what he was doing. He said that the younger brother, Ephraim, would be greater than Manasseh, even though Manasseh would also become a great people.

2. To carry the sins of others

(a) Laying hands on animals

Even animals were set aside for a particular purpose by the laying on of hands.

In preparation for the consecration of Aaron and his sons as priests, the Lord instructed Moses to get ready a young bull and two rams without blemish, together with unleavened bread, unleavened cakes mixed with oil and unleavened wafers anointed with oil.

On the day of the consecration, at the tabernacle of meeting, Aaron and his sons were first washed with water. Then Aaron was dressed in priestly garments and anointing oil was poured on his head. After that, his sons were dressed in their tunics, and then they were all girded with sashes and hats were put on their heads.

As part of the consecration, the bull and two rams were sacrificed. Aaron and his sons were required to put their hands on the heads of each of these animals in turn:

> *"You shall also take one ram, and Aaron and his sons shall put their hands on the head of the ram ... "*   (Exodus 29:15)

The bull became a sin offering and its blood was placed on the horns of the altar and beside the base of the altar.

After Aaron and his sons had laid hands on the head of one of the rams, it was slaughtered, and then its blood was sprinkled all around the altar, and the remainder of the animal was burnt on the altar as an offering to the Lord.

In the case of the other ram, Aaron and his sons had to lay their hands on it before it too was slaughtered. Then Moses was required to take some of its blood and put it on the tip of the right ear of Aaron and of each of his sons and on the thumb of their right hand and on the big toe of their right foot and sprinkle the blood around the altar. In addition, some of the blood was sprinkled on Aaron and his sons' garments. In that way, he, his sons and their garments would be hallowed.

Before the blood of these animals could be used for the above purposes, hands had to be laid on their heads. In this way these animals were set aside for the particular purpose for which they were intended, namely the process of consecration.

Scripture sets out this event as follows:

"Then Moses took some of the anointing oil and some of the blood which was on the altar, and sprinkled it on Aaron, on his garments, on his sons, and on the garments of his sons with him; and he consecrated Aaron, his garments, his sons, and the garments of his sons with him." (Leviticus 8:30)

(b) Day of Atonement

Leviticus 16 sets out the procedure for the Day of Atonement, which is one of the most significant days in the Jewish calendar.

Its significance lies primarily in the fact that it prefigures the entry of Jesus Christ as the High Priest, into heaven itself.

Aaron was required to offer a bull as a sin offering in order to make atonement for himself and for his house.

Then he was required to take two goats and present them before the Lord at the door of the tabernacle of meeting.

After that, he had to cast lots for the two goats, one lot for the Lord and the other for the scapegoat.

The goat upon which the Lord's lot fell was then offered as a sin offering, but the goat which was to become the scapegoat was presented alive before the Lord. After the atonement had been made it was released into the wilderness as the scapegoat.

Aaron was required to take some of the bull's blood and sprinkle it with his finger on the east side of the mercy seat. Then he did the same thing seven times in front of the mercy seat. He then had to kill the goat which was the sin offering of the people and sprinkle its blood along with the bull's blood seven times on the horns of the altar in the Most Holy Place.

This ceremony took place only once a year. When Aaron went in to make atonement in the Holy Place, there was to be no one in the tabernacle of meeting. Nor was there to be anybody there when he came out.

If he went into the Holy Place at any other time, he would die. God promised that on that day, when he carried out his duties in the Holiest of Holies He would appear in a cloud above the mercy seat.

Aaron was required to make atonement for the children of Israel because of their uncleanness and their transgressions. By offering the blood of the bull and the goat he was making atonement for sins which both he and the people had committed in ignorance.

Now Jesus Christ, as our High Priest, has risen from the dead and He Himself has gone into the Holiest of Holies in the heavens, not with the blood of goats or calves, but with His own blood: now He is Mediator of the new covenant. Thus, it is no longer necessary for the sacrifice of animals to take place and for the High Priest to enter an earthly tabernacle to atone for the sins of the people.

A second aspect, however, is also extremely important:

> *"Aaron shall lay both his hands on the head of the live goat, confess over it all the iniquities of the children of Israel, and all their transgressions, concerning all their sins, putting them on the head of the goat, and shall send it away into the wilderness by the hand of a suitable man. The goat shall bear on itself all their iniquities to an uninhabited land; and he shall release the goat in the wilderness."*   (Leviticus 16:21–22)

As Aaron laid his hands on the head of the live goat, all the sins and transgressions of the children of Israel were put on its head so that when it was sent out into the wilderness to an uninhabited land it took their sins with it.

This is a picture of Jesus Christ on the cross. As He hung on the cross, set aside by God Himself for this purpose, He took upon Himself all our sins and iniquities:

> *"He shall see the labor of His soul, and be satisfied.*
> *By His knowledge My righteous Servant shall justify many,*
> *For He shall bear their iniquities.*
> *Therefore I will divide Him a portion with the great,*
> *And He shall divide the spoil with the strong,*
> *Because He poured out His soul unto death,*
> *And He was numbered with the transgressors,*
> *And He bore the sin of many,*
> *And made intercession for the transgressors."*
>
> (Isaiah 53:11–12)

Just as the live goat was set aside for the purpose of carrying the sins of the people, so Jesus Christ Himself was set aside as a sin offering to bear our sins. The sins of Israel were placed on the head of the live goat by the laying on of hands. In the case of Jesus Christ, He voluntarily took upon Himself all of our sins and iniquities.

(c) Carrying their own sins

However, not all sins could be dealt with in this way. In Leviticus the story is told of a man, whose mother was an

Israelite and whose father was an Egyptian, who began to blaspheme the name of the Lord and curse Him. God told Moses that this person was to be taken outside of the camp where all who had heard him blaspheme were to lay their hands on his head, and then the congregation was to stone him.

In this way, it was made clear that this man would bear his own sin. No atonement could be made for him:

> *"Take outside the camp him who has cursed; then let all who heard him lay their hands on his head, and let all the congregation stone him."* (Leviticus 24:14)

3. To set apart for service

(a) Aaron and his sons

Following the consecration of Aaron and his sons for their priestly duties God instructed Moses to bring the whole tribe of Levi before Him so they could be set apart for their role of serving in the tabernacle. On the day that the Lord killed all the first-born of the Egyptians, before the Israelites were released from their captivity, God had decreed that He had set apart the first-born of the children of Israel, both man and beast, for Himself. Now, He was giving the Levites back as a gift to Aaron and his sons to work in the tabernacle of meeting but first they needed to be set apart and to be cleansed.

In the presence of the Lord, all the children of Israel laid their hands on the Levites:

> *"So you shall bring the Levites before the LORD, and the children of Israel shall lay their hands on the Levites ... "*
> (Numbers 8:10)

Then, in turn, the Levites had to lay their hands on the heads of two young bulls, one of which had to be offered as a sin offering and the other as a burnt offering, in order to make atonement for them:

> *"Then the Levites shall lay their hands on the heads of the young bulls, and you shall offer one as a sin offering and the other as a burnt offering to the LORD, to make atonement for the Levites."* (Numbers 8:12)

As well as serving in the tabernacle of meeting, their function was to make atonement for the children of Israel so that there would be no plague among them:

> *"And I have given the Levites as a gift to Aaron and his sons from among the children of Israel, to do the work for the children of Israel in the tabernacle of meeting, and to make atonement for the children of Israel, that there be no plague among the children of Israel when the children of Israel come near the sanctuary."*
>
> (Numbers 8:19)

In these examples, hands were laid both upon the Levites to consecrate them for service and upon the animals so that they could become sin offerings for the Levites.

(b) Joshua

When the time of Moses' death approached, he asked the Lord to appoint a new leader for the congregation of Israel. The Lord told him to lay his hands on Joshua, the son of Nun, a man in whom was the Holy Spirit, to set him apart for service as the leader of the congregation. Moses did so:

> *"And he laid his hands on him and inaugurated him, just as the* Lord *commanded by the hand of Moses."*   (Numbers 27:23)

Deuteronomy 34:9 also records this event:

> *"Now Joshua the son of Nun was full of the spirit of wisdom, for Moses had laid his hands on him; so the children of Israel heeded him, and did as the* Lord *had commanded Moses."*

By laying hands on Joshua, Moses passed on to him some of the giftings, including wisdom and courage, which he himself had received from God. He also made it clear that Joshua was now the leader who was to continue his office after him.

On this occasion, there was not only the setting aside for service, but there was an impartation of a gift. As a result of Moses laying his hands on him Joshua became full of the spirit of wisdom.

Summary

The purposes of the laying on of hands are:

1. To impart a blessing.

2. To carry the sins of others.

   Examples:
   (a) animals;
   (b) the Day of Atonement;
   (c) a person being required carry his own sin.

3. To set aside for service.

   Examples:
   (a) Aaron and his sons;
   (b) Joshua.

Chapter 17

Why We Should Do It

1. Jesus Christ the sin offering

Now that Jesus Christ has carried our sins, it is no longer necessary for us to lay hands on animals so that they may carry our sins. Jesus has become our sin offering or sin bearer.

2. Laying hands on others to impart a blessing

Jesus Christ laid hands on others to impart a blessing:

> "Then little children were brought to Him that He might put His hands on them and pray, but the disciples rebuked them. But Jesus said, 'Let the little children come to Me, and do not forbid them; for of such is the kingdom of heaven.' And He laid His hands on them and departed from there."
>
> (Matthew 19:13–15)

3. To give healing

The people of Jesus' day obviously understood that, by the laying on of hands, Jesus could impart the gift of healing to a person.

(a) Jairus and his daughter

This is illustrated by the story of Jairus, who begged Jesus to lay hands on his little daughter:

> "and begged Him earnestly, saying, 'My little daughter lies at the point of death. Come and lay Your hands on her, that she may be healed, and she will live.'"
>
> (Mark 5:23)

Although, by the time Jesus got to the child, she had already died, Jesus took her by the hands and raised her from the dead:

> *"Then He took the child by the hand, and said to her, 'Talitha, cumi,' which is translated, 'Little girl, I say to you, arise.' Immediately the girl arose and walked, for she was twelve years of age. And they were overcome with great amazement."*
>
> (Mark 5:41–42)

Thus, He imparted the gift of life to her as a healing miracle.

In the very next chapter of Mark's Gospel, we read one of the most amazing statements in the New Testament:

> *"Now He could do no mighty work there, except that He laid His hands on a few sick people and healed them."*   (Mark 6:5)

Jesus' ability to do miracles was restricted by their unbelief. This fact clearly demonstrates the need for belief when we pray for the sick; unbelief quenches the Holy Spirit.

(b) Healing of the blind man

The blind man was healed after Jesus had spat on his eyes and put His hands on him:

> *"So He took the blind man by the hand and led him out of the town. And when He had spit on his eyes and put His hands on him, He asked him if he saw anything."*   (Mark 8:23)

(c) Jesus heals all

On another occasion Jesus laid hands on every one of the people and healed them:

> *"When the sun was setting, all those who had any that were sick with various diseases brought them to Him; and He laid His hands on every one of them and healed them."*   (Luke 4:40)

(d) Demons flee

As He did so, demons came out of many of those who were healed. This demonstrates something which many of us who are involved in the healing ministry find to be true today, namely that unless we are involved in the casting out of demons when we pray for the sick, we will not achieve the best results.

*"And demons also came out of many, crying out and saying,
'You are the Christ, the Son of God!' And He, rebuking them, did
not allow them to speak, for they knew that He was the Christ."*
(Luke 4:41)

On another occasion, Jesus laid hands on a woman for healing,
who had been bound by Satan for eighteen years. Even though
she was a daughter of Abraham, Satan had afflicted her. In the
same way today, we find that many Christians are afflicted by
demonic power and need to be loosed from this bondage in
order to be healed.

*"So ought not this woman, being a daughter of Abraham, whom
Satan has bound – think of it – for eighteen years, be loosed from
this bond on the Sabbath?"*   (Luke 13:16)

4. Authority of believers for the laying on of hands

All believers in Jesus Christ have been given authority to lay
hands on the sick and expect that they will recover:

*"And these signs will follow those who believe: In My name they
will cast out demons; they will speak with new tongues; they will
take up serpents; and if they drink anything deadly, it will by no
means hurt them; they will lay hands on the sick, and they will
recover."*   (Mark 16:17–18)

Jesus Christ has clearly given us this authority and, as we obey
with faith, we will always see tremendous results. If the correct
conditions pertain, namely belief in God and true repentance,
the anointing of God is present for healing.

Thus, we have been given the authority to lay hands on the
sick so they will recover. This is another aspect of the impartation of gifts by the laying on of hands.

5. Authority of the elders of the church

James authorizes the elders of a church to anoint the sick and
believe for their healing:

*"Is anyone among you sick? Let him call for the elders of the
church, and let them pray over him, anointing him with oil in
the name of the Lord. And the prayer of faith will save the sick,*

and the Lord will raise him up. And if he has committed sins, he
will be forgiven."   (James 5:14–15)

As an evangelist, I find frequently that people go to the doctor
first rather than to God. I believe that, through the grace of
God, the medical profession has much to offer. In no way
would I seek to denigrate the skills of these dedicated men and
women. However, I believe we should follow the scriptural
injunction and look to the Lord first for healing.

It is clear that the above scripture in James is referring to
believers. It is proper for them to go to the elders of the church
and let them pray over them and anoint them with oil in the
name of the Lord. Through the prayer of faith the Lord will raise
the sick person up, and if he has committed sins he will be
forgiven.

The next scripture indicates the importance of confession:

"Confess your trespasses to one another, and pray for one
another, that you may be healed. The effective, fervent prayer
of a righteous man avails much."   (James 5:16)

The confession of sins forms a vital part of the healing ministry.
As we confess any sins of which we are aware to the elders and
let them anoint us with oil, then God's healing power can flow
in a mighty way.

For the person who is not a Christian but comes to an
evangelistic meeting, anointing with oil is not always appropriate. However, the laying on of hands is perfectly appropriate
and, as God's power moves through such a person, then they
will recognize the almighty love and power of God.

In evangelistic meetings I notice that when unbelievers are
called out as a result of a word of knowledge and hands are laid
on them for healing, they invariably respond to the call for
salvation. They have sensed the love and anointing of God.

Many Christians disobey James 5:14. They will often come to
an evangelist such as myself rather than go to the elders of their
church. This is not the scriptural order. We should always seek
help from the elders of our church.

The oil itself does not have any healing properties. However,
it is a symbol of the Holy Spirit and encourages belief in the
person for whom prayer is being offered. As the prayer of faith is
uttered by one or more of the elders, then the anointing of the

Holy Spirit is felt and those present recognize that God is in their midst for healing.

Such a prayer of faith could be as follows:

> "Dear Heavenly Father, in Jesus Christ's name, I pray for Your healing love to fall now on ....
> In the name of Jesus Christ, we rebuke every form of sickness afflicting this person and command any demonic power of sickness to flee now in Jesus Christ's name. We thank You, dear Lord, for healing our dear brother/sister. Thank You, Father, in Jesus' name. Amen."

6. Laying hands on the unbeliever

There is scriptural evidence that in New Testament times hands were laid on unbelievers and by the grace of God they were healed:

> *"And it happened that the father of Publius lay sick of a fever and dysentery. Paul went in to him and prayed, and he laid his hands on him and healed him."* (Acts 28:8)

7. Healing and miracles

It should be noted that in Mark 16:18 the words are used, *"they will recover."* Sometimes this recovery is instantaneous, but very frequently it occurs over a period of time. It is therefore important for the person who has sought prayer for healing to continue to believe after prayer, even though nothing seems to have happened.

I often encourage people to be prayed for by their church eldership on more than one occasion. I do not take the view that this act indicates lack of faith if both that person and the elders continue truly to believe. By the continual laying on of hands, the faith of the person grows and he or she is encouraged to believe in a greater depth for healing. However, this must not become a mechanical approach but must at all times be done with the utmost faith in the healing love of God.

If healing does occur instantly, then it is an evidence of the gift of miracles. Many times in evangelistic meetings I am privileged to see a person healed instantly. On other occasions people find as they walk out of the meeting that they have, in fact, been healed. Others experience their healing a few days later.

Quite frequently, after people have known their healing, some of the symptoms appear to return and it is then that they must stand firm in their faith. I have heard many testimonies from people who have known their healing, but then there has been a recurrence of symptoms. However, as they have stood firm in their faith and rebuked the spirit of sickness attacking them, they have finally known complete and absolute healing.

When hands have been laid upon somebody, I encourage them to begin to thank God for their healing, even before it appears. As the word of God says:

> *"Jesus said to her, 'Did I not say to you that if you would believe you would see the glory of God?'"* (John 11:40)

Often we have to believe before we see the effect of God working in our body. The healing may be taking place although the symptoms are still present. As we continue to believe, then the symptoms will completely disappear.

When I pray for people to be healed who are on medication, I encourage them not to stop their medication without consulting their doctor. I ask them to tell their doctor that they believe that they are being healed by God and request that the medication be reduced. Most doctors are only too willing to see their patients receiving less medication and are usually very cooperative. As they are able to monitor the patient's progress during the healing process, then God can be glorified.

8. Faith and presumption

There is a narrow line between faith and presumption. As we move in true faith, then we can have confidence that God is involved in our healing. During this period it can be a time for self-examination and of repentance from any sin which could be hindering the healing. We have an opportunity to listen to the voice of the Lord and read His word.

Presumption, however, has the opposite effect. We presume we are healed and do not give the Holy Spirit an opportunity to speak to us in correcting love. In that way we can miss our healing.

I know of many testimonies of people who, as they have firmly held their faith in the healing power of God and responded to His will, have found their healing occur over a period of time. Others have known instant, miraculous healing. However, whichever way God heals, let us give Him the glory.

9. Further signs and wonders

In the early Church, we see signs and wonders being done among the people as the apostles laid hands on them:

> *"And through the hands of the apostles many signs and wonders were done among the people. And they were all with one accord in Solomon's Porch."*   (Acts 5:12)

10. The laying on of hands for service

It is clear that the early Church regarded the laying on of hands as an important method in the commissioning of elders and of ministries.

As the early Church began to grow, the twelve apostles wanted to be able to devote themselves completely to prayer and the ministry of the word of God. Therefore, it was suggested that seven men of good reputation, full of the Holy Spirit and wisdom, should be appointed to look after practical tasks such as serving at tables.

Seven such men were chosen and then, after prayer, the apostles laid their hands on them to set them apart for service:

> *"whom they set before the apostles; and when they had prayed, they laid hands on them."*   (Acts 6:6)

We find a similar scripture in Acts 13:

> *"Now in the church that was at Antioch there were certain prophets and teachers: Barnabas, Simeon who was called Niger, Lucius of Cyrene, Manaen who had been brought up with Herod the tetrarch, and Saul. As they ministered to the Lord and fasted, the Holy Spirit said, 'Now separate to Me Barnabas and Saul for the work to which I have called them.' Then, having fasted and prayed, and laid hands on them, they sent them away."*
>   (Acts 13:1–3)

From this scripture it is clear that the early Church practiced the laying on of hands in order to set apart individuals for service. This, however, was only done after fasting and praying by the church.

When we fast, we set aside the desires of the flesh. Our body wants to continue to receive physical food and often this desire will subjugate our spiritual desires. By disciplining our body, we find that our spirit is more open to the power of God.

Just as hands were laid on Joshua by Moses in order to make it clear to everybody that God had empowered Joshua to go out and lead the nation of Israel after the death of Moses, similarly, the laying on of hands on the elders signifies a public accept- ance of their ministry.

As Paul and Barnabas traveled and preached the gospel, they appointed elders:

> *"And when they had preached the gospel to that city and made many disciples, they returned to Lystra, Iconium, and Antioch, strengthening the souls of the disciples, exhorting them to continue in the faith, and saying, 'We must through many tribulations enter the kingdom of God.' So when they had appointed elders in every church, and prayed with fasting, they commended them to the Lord in whom they had believed."*
>
> (Acts 14:21–23)

It is clear from this scripture that great care was taken in the appointment of elders.

11. The laying on of hands to impart the Holy Spirit

We now see a new aspect of the laying on of hands appearing in Scripture.

(a) Philip in Samaria
As we have already seen (p. 110), when Philip had gone down to Samaria and preached Jesus Christ to the Samaritans, great signs and wonders had taken place. The evidence of the work of the Holy Spirit in the lives of the new believers, after the apostles had come and laid hands on them, evoked a desire in Simon the sorcerer to have what they had:

> *"And when Simon saw that through the laying on of the apostles' hands the Holy Spirit was given, he offered them money ..."* (Acts 8:18)

(b) Saul on the Damascus road
The following dialogue took place between Saul and the Lord on the Damascus road:

> *"So he, trembling and astonished, said, 'Lord, what do You want me to do?' Then the Lord said to him, 'Arise and go into the city, and you will be told what you must do.'"* (Acts 9:6)

When he reached Damascus, after three days he was visited by a disciple named Ananias whom the Lord had told in a vision to go to the house of Judas and ask for Saul of Tarsus. This is what happened next:

> *"And Ananias went his way and entered the house; and laying his hands on him he said, 'Brother Saul, the Lord Jesus, who appeared to you on the road as you came, has sent me that you may receive your sight and be filled with the Holy Spirit.'"*
>
> (Acts 9:17)

And so, Saul was filled with the Holy Spirit by the laying on of hands. Later, of course, his name was changed to Paul.

Some years later, when Paul came to Ephesus and found disciples who had not been baptized with the Holy Spirit, he laid hands on them with similar results:

> *"And when Paul had laid hands on them, the Holy Spirit came upon them, and they spoke with tongues and prophesied."*
>
> (Acts 19:6)

It is clear, then, that one of the ways in which we can receive the Holy Spirit, is by the laying on of hands. However, it is not the only way.

12. The laying on of hands to receive the gifts of the Holy Spirit

There are nine spiritual gifts of the Holy Spirit referred to in 1 Corinthians 12. They are:

- the word of wisdom
- the word of knowledge
- the gift of faith
- the gifts of healing
- the working of miracles
- the gift of prophecy
- the discerning of spirits
- different kinds of tongues
- interpretation of tongues

In the case of five of these, namely the word of wisdom, the word of knowledge, prophecy, the discerning of spirits and interpretation of tongues, they can be described as God speaking to us audibly or by vision or by thought or impression. As we listen to Him in this way, we are able to minister in these gifts.

The word of wisdom tells us how to deal with a person or situation, while the word of knowledge tells us about a person or situation.

The discerning of spirits is a gift whereby we discern spiritual powers which are not of God operating around or through another person. The interpretation of tongues involves the public interpretation of a tongue already spoken out in a meeting.

The gifts of faith, healings, miracles, and tongues are gifts of God given directly to believers to enable them to manifest God's power and love as the Holy Spirit leads.

I have elaborated upon these gifts further in my books, *Receiving the Gifts of the Holy Spirit, Demons Defeated* and *How to Cast Out Demons and Break Curses.*

One of the ways in which these gifts can be imparted is by the laying on of hands. Thus, we find Paul writing to Timothy:

> *"Do not neglect the gift that is in you, which was given to you by prophecy with the laying on of the hands of the eldership."*
> (1 Timothy 4:14)

Again, in his second letter to Timothy, Paul reminds Timothy to stir up the gift of God which he had received through the laying on of Paul's hands:

> *"Therefore I remind you to stir up the gift of God which is in you through the laying on of my hands."*   (2 Timothy 1:6)

Paul indirectly refers to these gifts again in 1 Timothy 1:18:

> *"This charge I commit to you, son Timothy, according to the prophecies previously made concerning you, that by them you may wage the good warfare ... "*

It is clear that Timothy received a spiritual gift from Paul through the laying on of hands. Although we are not told what this gift was, it is clear that its purpose was the building up of the body of Christ.

In the first scripture, the gift was given by the laying on of hands by the elders, accompanied by prophecy. Frequently, when we are laying hands on people to receive gifts, the Holy Spirit gives us a clear word of prophecy, that is a word of edification, exhortation and comfort, to encourage the person receiving the gift.

Timothy was obviously commissioned by the elders to carry out his ministry which included evangelism. In the course of this commissioning, the Lord gave words of prophecy through the elders to encourage him in his walk with Him.

13. Spiritual warfare

Paul refers to the waging of warfare. Every Christian who begins to move in the power of God finds themselves engaged in this warfare, as the following scripture emphasizes:

> *"For we do not wrestle against flesh and blood, but against principalities, against powers, against the rulers of the darkness of this age, against spiritual hosts of wickedness in the heavenly places."*   (Ephesians 6:12)

When we begin to step out for the Lord, then we find that there are unseen spiritual powers which seek to resist us. That is why the gift of faith is so important and, similarly, the gift of discerning of spirits. As we begin to discern the spiritual powers operating against us, then we are able to deal more effectively with them in the name of Jesus Christ. Paul reminds us how to combat these spiritual powers:

> *"Therefore take up the whole armor of God, that you may be able to withstand in the evil day, and having done all, to stand. Stand therefore, having girded your waist with truth, having put on the breastplate of righteousness, and having shod your feet with the preparation of the gospel of peace; above all, taking the shield of faith with which you will be able to quench all the fiery darts of the wicked one. And take the helmet of salvation, and the sword of the Spirit, which is the word of God; praying always with all prayer and supplication in the Spirit, being watchful to this end with all perseverance and supplication for all the saints ... "*   (Ephesians 6:13–18)

14. Caution

We are given the following caution concerning the laying on of hands:

> *"Do not lay hands on anyone hastily, nor share in other people's sins; keep yourself pure."* (1 Timothy 5:22)

While this can include taking care in the appointment of elders or deacons, nevertheless it also refers to the laying on of hands generally. It is particularly important never to fall into the danger of sharing in other people's sins.

On occasions, when we come to lay hands upon people, we discern that there are spiritual powers within them that are not of God. Similarly, we ourselves may be under some form of spiritual attack.

Therefore, when we lay hands on others, we should be aware of the cleansing power of the blood of Jesus and claim the protection of that blood. Whenever I am engaged in public teaching seminars during the course of which I encourage people to lay hands on others, I always ensure that we first plead the blood of Jesus Christ. By pleading the blood, we are reminding Satan, who accuses us before God day and night, that we have been cleansed, redeemed, sanctified and justified by the blood of Jesus Christ and that, accordingly, as we walk before the Lord in holiness and righteousness, the enemy cannot attack us.

> *"And they overcame him by the blood of the Lamb and by the word of their testimony, and they did not love their lives to the death."* (Revelation 12:11)

Summary

The New Testament makes the following clear:

1. Since Jesus Christ has become our sin-bearer and died on the cross for us, it is no longer necessary to lay hands on animals to carry our sins or for persons themselves to bear their own sins.

2. Jesus Christ laid hands on the sick, both to bless them and heal them.

3. All believers have been commissioned to lay hands on the sick so that they may recover.

4. We have the apostolic pattern of the apostles laying hands on the sick for their recovery.

5. There is the clear precedent in Scripture for the laying on of hands to receive the baptism with the Holy Spirit.

6. The gifts of the Holy Spirit are imparted through the laying on of hands.

7. People are set apart for service by the laying on of hands. For example, the apostles laid hands on the seven deacons.

8. The following three reasons can thus be established for the laying on of hands:
   (a) to set an individual apart for service for God;
   (b) to receive the baptism with the Holy Spirit;
   (c) to impart the gifts of the Holy Spirit, including baptism with the Holy Spirit.

Chapter 18

What Happens When We Die?

We turn now to the fifth of the doctrines outlined in Hebrews 6:1–2, the resurrection of the dead.

It is perfectly clear from Scripture that no one has power over the human spirit to retain it at the time of death, and that no one has power over death:

> *"No one has power over the spirit to retain the spirit,*
> *And no one has power in the day of death.*
> *There is no release from that war,*
> *And wickedness will not deliver those who are given to it."*
>
> (Ecclesiastes 8:8)

Many people claim to have had partial death experiences when their spirit has floated above their body and they have looked down and seen doctors resuscitating them. However, when death does finally happen, Scripture refers to the *"silver cord"* being *"loosed"* and the spirit returning to God who gave it:

> *"Remember your Creator before the silver cord is loosed,*
> *Or the golden bowl is broken,*
> *Or the pitcher shattered at the fountain,*
> *Or the wheel broken at the well.*
> *Then the dust will return to the earth as it was,*
> *And the spirit will return to God who gave it."*
>
> (Ecclesiastes 12:6–7)

There is nothing in the word of God to justify the claim that the spirits of the dead stay around on this earth as ghosts seeking rest. This is a belief of Buddhism and other eastern religions.

It is quite clear that the human spirit returns to God who gave it.

The dead are aware of their existence

Various scriptures make it clear to us that the dead are aware of their existence. Thus, in Isaiah 14, we are told the fate of the King of Babylon who had acted harshly against the Jews:

> *"Hell from beneath is excited about you,*
> *To meet you at your coming;*
> *It stirs up the dead for you,*
> *All the chief ones of the earth;*
> *It has raised up from their thrones*
> *All the kings of the nations.*
> *They all shall speak and say to you:*
> *'Have you also become as weak as we?*
> *Have you become like us?*
> *Your pomp is brought down to Sheol,*
> *And the sound of your stringed instruments;*
> *The maggot is spread under you,*
> *And worms cover you.'"*   (Isaiah 14:9–11)

We are also given an insight into what will happen to Satan when he is finally cast into the pit:

> *"How you are fallen from heaven,*
> *O Lucifer, son of the morning!*
> *How you are cut down to the ground,*
> *You who weakened the nations!*
> *For you have said in your heart:*
> *'I will ascend into heaven,*
> *I will exalt my throne above the stars of God;*
> *I will also sit on the mount of the congregation*
> *On the farthest sides of the north;*
> *I will ascend above the heights of the clouds,*
> *I will be like the Most High.'*
> *Yet you shall be brought down to Sheol,*
> *To the lowest depths of the Pit.*
>
> *Those who see you will gaze at you,*
> *And consider you, saying:*
> *'Is this the man who made the earth tremble,*
> *Who shook kingdoms,*
> *Who made the world as a wilderness*
> *And destroyed its cities,*
> *Who did not open the house of his prisoners?'"*

(Isaiah 14:12–17)

Ezekiel, too, lifts the curtain on the scene after death:

> *"Son of man, wail over the multitude of Egypt,*
> *And cast them down to the depths of the earth,*
> *Her and the daughters of the famous nations,*
> *With those who go down to the Pit:*
> *'Whom do you surpass in beauty?*
> *Go down, be placed with the uncircumcised.'"*
>
> (Ezekiel 32:18–19)

These passages make it clear both that the departed dead recognize one another and that they can be recognized. In the last quotation Ezekiel refers to four nations among the dead, namely Assyria, Elam, Meshech and Tubal, Edom, as well as to the mighty ancient ruler of Egypt, Pharoah. Later in the chapter he speaks of Assyria:

> *"Assyria is there, and all her company,*
> *With their graves all around her,*
> *All of them slain, fallen by the sword.*
> *Her graves are set in the recesses of the Pit,*
> *And her company is all around her grave,*
> *All of them slain, fallen by the sword,*
> *Who caused terror in the land of the living."*
>
> (Ezekiel 32:22–23)

Separation of the righteous and unrighteous dead

Scripture indicates a separation of the righteous dead from the unrighteous. In His parable concerning the rich man and the beggar named Lazarus Jesus paints a very revealing picture of their separation following their deaths:

> *"So it was that the beggar died, and was carried by the angels to Abraham's bosom. The rich man also died and was buried. And being in torments in Hades, he lifted up his eyes and saw Abraham afar off, and Lazarus in his bosom. Then he cried and said, 'Father Abraham, have mercy on me, and send Lazarus that he may dip the tip of his finger in water and cool my tongue; for I am tormented in this flame.' But Abraham said, 'Son, remember that in your lifetime you received your good things, and likewise Lazarus evil things; but now he is comforted and you are tormented. And besides all this, between us and you*

there is a great gulf fixed, so that those who want to pass from here to you cannot, nor can those from there pass to us.'"

(Luke 16:22–26)

Before Jesus Christ died on the cross and rose from the dead, it seems from Scripture that the departed dead went to Hades, the place of departed spirits. The only exceptions were some Old Testament saints like Enoch and Elijah. That place was clearly divided into two areas, namely:

1.   a part described as 'Abraham's bosom'
2.   a place of torment.

Summary

1.   No one has power over the spirit to retain it on this earth.

2.   The dead are aware of their existence.

3.   At death, the righteous and unrighteous dead are separated.

4.   Hades is divided into two places: one described as 'Abraham's bosom' and the other a place of torment.

5.   Before the death and resurrection of Jesus Christ, the righteous dead went to 'Abraham's bosom' while the unrighteous dead went to the place of torment.

Chapter 19

Resurrection

The word "resurrection" means the act of coming back to life after death or the state of those who have returned to life.

Job's faith

In the book of Job we have a bold statement of faith made by Job concerning his resurrection:

> *"For I know that my Redeemer lives,*
> *And He shall stand at last on the earth;*
> *And after my skin is destroyed, this I know,*
> *That in my flesh I shall see God,*
> *Whom I shall see for myself,*
> *And my eyes shall behold, and not another.*
> *How my heart yearns within me!"*   (Job 19:25–27)

Clearly Job had faith that one day, in his flesh, he would see God.
   Psalm 22 contains another prophecy of resurrection:

> *"All the prosperous of the earth*
> *Shall eat and worship;*
> *All those who go down to the dust*
> *Shall bow before Him,*
> *Even he who cannot keep himself alive."*   (Psalm 22:29)

This scripture confirms that one day everybody will be resurrected to bow down before God.
   Psalm 71 contains a Messianic prophecy:

> *"You, who have shown me great and severe troubles,*
> *Shall revive me again,*

> *And bring me up again from the depths of the earth.*
> *You shall increase my greatness,*
> *And comfort me on every side."*   (Psalm 71:20–21)

This is a prophecy about Jesus Christ and His crucifixion. It tells of His descent into the depths of Sheol or Hades, the place where the spirits of the dead were sent, and prophecies that He would be revived again and brought up from Sheol in His resurrection. At that time He would be restored to His throne of grace beside God and would receive great comfort on every side.

Peter's sermon

On the Day of Pentecost, Peter quoted Psalm 16 as evidence of the resurrection of Jesus Christ:

> *"I have set the* Lord *always before me;*
> *Because He is at my right hand I shall not be moved.*
> *Therefore my heart is glad, and my glory rejoices;*
> *My flesh also will rest in hope.*
> *For You will not leave my soul in Sheol,*
> *Nor will You allow Your Holy One to see corruption.*
> *You will show me the path of life;*
> *In Your presence is fullness of joy;*
> *At Your right hand are pleasures forevermore."*
>
> (Psalm 16:8–11)

This is a specific prophecy concerning the Lord Himself, given through the lips of David. Peter went on to say:

> *"He, foreseeing this, spoke concerning the resurrection of the Christ, that His soul was not left in Hades, nor did His flesh see corruption."*   (Acts 2:31)

We can conclude from this that when Jesus Christ was crucified, His soul (including His spirit) went into Sheol, but His mortal body was left on earth and did not suffer corruption. There were over five hundred witnesses to His resurrection:

> *"This Jesus God has raised up, of which we are all witnesses. Therefore being exalted to the right hand of God, and having received from the Father the promise of the Holy Spirit, He poured out this which you now see and hear."*
>
> (Acts 2:32–33)

"After that He was seen by over five hundred brethren at once,
of whom the greater part remain to the present, but some have
fallen asleep." (1 Corinthians 15:6)

Isaiah is confident of resurrection

In Isaiah 26 we find the following statement:

"Your dead shall live;
Together with my dead body they shall arise.
Awake and sing, you who dwell in dust;
For your dew is like the dew of herbs,
And the earth shall cast out the dead." (Isaiah 26:19)

Isaiah expresses similar confidence to that expressed by Job,
namely that the dead shall live and he, with them, will arise.

Obviously, those who do the singing are the righteous dead.

Daniel's prophecy

The book of Daniel contains the following prophecy:

"At that time Michael shall stand up,
The great prince who stands watch over the sons of your
    people;
And there shall be a time of trouble,
Such as never was since there was a nation,
Even to that time.
And at that time your people shall be delivered,
Every one who is found written in the book.
And many of those who sleep in the dust of the earth shall
    awake,
Some to everlasting life,
Some to shame and everlasting contempt.
Those who are wise shall shine
Like the brightness of the firmament.
And those who turn many to righteousness
Like the stars forever and ever." (Daniel 12:1–3)

"Sons of your people" refers to the people of Israel.

This is a prophecy about the end times when there will be *"a*
time of trouble," spoken of elsewhere as *"the coming time of*
tribulation." However, it promises that the people of Israel will

be delivered, in particular everyone whose name is written in the Book of Life.

Daniel also alludes to the resurrection of the righteous dead and makes it clear that they will be separated from the unrighteous dead. They will arise to everlasting life, while the unrighteous dead will face shame and everlasting contempt.

Those who are wise, namely those who during their lifetime have obeyed the Lord, will shine *"like the brightness of the firmament."* But for those who have led others to turn to righteousness there is greater glory: they will shine *"like the stars forever and ever."*

Hosea's prophecy

In Hosea we find the following prophecy:

> *"Come, and let us return to the LORD;*
> *For He has torn, but He will heal us;*
> *He has stricken, but He will bind us up.*
> *After two days He will revive us;*
> *On the third day He will raise us up,*
> *That we may live in His sight.*
> *Let us know,*
> *Let us pursue the knowledge of the LORD.*
> *His going forth is established as the morning;*
> *He will come to us like the rain,*
> *Like the latter and former rain to the earth."*   (Hosea 6:1–3)

This clearly refers to the resurrection of Jesus Christ and also to those who surrender their lives to Him in true repentance. There is a promise of healing and a promise of resurrection.

True followers go into God's presence immediately after death

We can also conclude from the words of Jesus that His true followers can expect to go into His presence immediately after death:

> *"Most assuredly, I say to you, he who hears My word and believes in Him who sent Me has everlasting life, and shall not come into judgment, but has passed from death into life."*

(John 5:24)

"But if the Spirit of Him who raised Jesus from the dead dwells in you, He who raised Christ from the dead will also give life to your mortal bodies through His Spirit who dwells in you."

(Romans 8:11)

The justified and unjustified dead

It is reasonable, therefore, to conclude that the unjustified dead are still in Hades, while the justified dead are in the presence of God.

Summary

1. Resurrection means the act of coming back to life after death or the state of those who have returned to life.

2. Job believed that one day, in his flesh, he would see God.

3. Jesus always believed that God was before Him and at His right hand.

4. The body of Jesus Christ did not suffer corruption.

5. Daniel prophesied that at the time of the end, many of those who *"sleep in the dust"* shall awake, some to everlasting life and some to shame and everlasting contempt.

6. The unjustified dead are still in Hades while the justified dead are in the presence of God.

7. Those who truly follow Jesus Christ and obey His word will not have to face judgment.

Chapter 20

Christ the Firstfruits

"For since by man came death, by Man also came the resur-rection of the dead. For as in Adam all die, even so in Christ all shall be made alive. But each one in his own order: Christ the firstfruits, afterward those who are Christ's at His coming. Then comes the end, when He delivers the kingdom to God the Father, when He puts an end to all rule and all authority and power. For He must reign till He has put all enemies under His feet."

(1 Corinthians 15:21–25)

Just as through Adam spiritual death came, so through Jesus Christ comes the resurrection of the dead. Jesus promised that everybody would be resurrected, some to a resurrection of life and others to a resurrection of condemnation.

"Do not marvel at this; for the hour is coming in which all who are in the graves will hear His voice and come forth – those who have done good, to the resurrection of life, and those who have done evil, to the resurrection of condemnation."   (John 5:28–29)

As the first to rise from the dead Christ is described in Scripture as *"the firstfruits."*

The sheaf

God told the Israelites, through His servant Moses, that the firstborn of their people and cattle were sacred to the Lord, as was also the first produce of their vineyards and of their land, including their grain, wine, wool, olive oil, and honey. The manner in which this was to be dealt with is set out in Leviticus 23:

146

> *"And the* L*ORD* *spoke to Moses, saying, 'Speak to the children of Israel, and say to them: "When you come into the land which I give to you, and reap its harvest, then you shall bring a sheaf of the firstfruits of your harvest to the priest. He shall wave the sheaf before the* L*ORD*, *to be accepted on your behalf; on the day after the Sabbath the priest shall wave it."' "*
>
> (Leviticus 23:9–11)

The *"sheaf of the firstfruits"* is a type of Jesus Christ rising from the dead. Just as Moses was told to wave a sheaf made out of the first ripe stalks of wheat before the Lord, so that it could be accepted on behalf of the children of Israel, so in Romans 4 we find:

> *"Who was delivered up because of our offences, and was raised because of our justification."* (Romans 4:25)

Jesus Christ was raised from the dead by the will of God, confirming His own righteousness and also that the believer might be justified before God.

It should be noted that the priest was to wave the sheaf on the day after the Sabbath, namely the first day of the week. This is the day on which Jesus Christ rose from the dead.

The remaining dead

This waving of the firstfruits of the harvest was a triumphant act as well as an act of worship, confirming that the remaining harvest would be safely brought in. For us, it is an assurance that, through Jesus Christ's resurrection, all the remaining dead will, in due course, be resurrected. We find the following scripture in John 12:

> *"Most assuredly, I say to you, unless a grain of wheat falls into the ground and dies, it remains alone; but if it dies, it produces much grain."* (John 12:24)

Here we have a picture of a grain of wheat falling into the ground, dying and then producing much grain. In the same way Jesus Christ, in one sense, had to fall into the ground and die. If He had remained there, no fruit would have resulted from His life, but by His resurrection from the dead He has fulfilled God's purposes and given us an assurance of His love for us. As we believe in the resurrection and in Jesus Christ Himself, so we become the "grain" produced as a result of His death and resurrection.

I often think back to the death of my brother, Keith, when he was aged five and I was eight years of age. It was through his premature death that my parents turned to Jesus Christ and, in due course, prayed for me. Many years later I was born again of the Spirit of God. I am sure that if that event had not occurred so early in my life with its consequent impact bringing home to me the fact of death, then I may not have been set upon the course of life on which I presently find myself, namely as an evangelist preaching the gospel of Jesus Christ.

As a result of the ministry which the Lord has given me, many thousands have turned to Jesus Christ.

The firstfruits of the resurrection

We note that when Jesus Christ rose from the dead, He did not rise on His own:

> *"And Jesus cried out again with a loud voice, and yielded up His spirit. Then, behold, the veil of the temple was torn in two from top to bottom; and the earth quaked, and the rocks were split, and the graves were opened; and many bodies of the saints who had fallen asleep were raised; and coming out of the graves after His resurrection, they went into the holy city and appeared to many."*   (Matthew 27:50–53)

The exact timing of these events is not specified but it is fair to surmise that the resurrection of these saints did not occur until after the resurrection of Jesus Christ.

Jesus Christ died a lonely death in the same way as a single grain falls into the ground and dies. When He arose from the dead, He was no longer on His own, but brought with Him the firstfruits of the resurrection.

There is no clear statement here that all the bodies of the past righteous dead were raised. However, it appears that many rose from the dead. Their resurrected bodies had similar attributes to those of Jesus, namely that they were able to appear and disappear without the limitations of a normal human being.

Jesus preached to the spirits in prison

Peter tells us what happened after Jesus committed His Spirit to God as He died on the cross:

> *"For Christ also suffered once for sins, the just for the unjust,*
> *that He might bring us to God, being put to death in the flesh but*
> *made alive by the Spirit, by whom also He went and preached to*
> *the spirits in prison, who formerly were disobedient, when once*
> *the Divine longsuffering of God waited in the days of Noah,*
> *while the ark was being prepared, in which a few, that is, eight*
> *souls, were saved through water."* (1 Peter 3:18–20)

From this scripture we can conclude that Jesus Christ proclaimed the good news of His death and coming resurrection to the disobedient who had been imprisoned in one part of Hades. Having taken the keys of Hades and death Jesus now proclaimed His victory:

> *"I am He who lives, and was dead, and behold, I am alive*
> *forevermore. Amen. And I have the keys of Hades and of Death."*
> (Revelation 1:18)

It is also clear that He proclaimed the good news to the righteous dead in paradise:

> *"For this reason the gospel was preached also to those who are*
> *dead, that they might be judged according to men in the flesh,*
> *but live according to God in the spirit."* (1 Peter 4:6)

Jesus ascends on high

Thus, Jesus Christ went from the place of paradise in Sheol where the spirits of the departed righteous were held to the part reserved for the spirits of the wicked.

In so doing He was fulfilling every part of the cross, taking upon Himself in full everything relating to sin, both spiritual and physical.

From there He ascended on high, taking with Him the righteous dead who had been held captive in Hades:

> *"Therefore He says:*
>
>   *'When He ascended on high,*
>   *He led captivity captive,*
>   *and gave gifts to men.'*
>
> *(Now this, 'He ascended' – what does it mean but that He also*
> *first descended into the lower parts of the earth? He who*
> *descended is also the One who ascended far above all the*
> *heavens, that He might fill all things.)"* (Ephesians 4:8–10)

Having descended into the lower parts of the earth, Jesus Christ is now ascended far above all the heavens and into heaven itself with the righteous dead.

> *"But God, who is rich in mercy, because of His great love with which He loved us, even when we were dead in trespasses, made us alive together with Christ (by grace you have been saved), and raised us up together, and made us sit together in the heavenly places in Christ Jesus ..."*   (Ephesians 2:4–6)

The cloud of witnesses

After His resurrection, Jesus Christ appeared to His disciples for forty days and then finally ascended into heaven. We then read the following:

> *"Now when He had spoken these things, while they watched, He was taken up, and a cloud received Him out of their sight."*
>   (Acts 1:9)

From the context it would seem that the cloud referred to here is a cloud of Old Testament saints.

We are told two angels stood by the disciples as they watched Jesus being taken up into heaven. They said:

> *"Men of Galilee, why do you stand gazing up into heaven? This same Jesus, who was taken up from you into heaven, will so come in like manner as you saw Him go into heaven."*   (Acts 1:11)

From this we can deduce that Jesus will return from heaven with clouds of His saints with Him.

The writer to the Hebrews speaks of believers being surrounded by a cloud of witnesses:

> *"Therefore we also, since we are surrounded by so great a cloud of witnesses, let us lay aside every weight, and the sin which so easily ensnares us, and let us run with endurance the race that is set before us ..."*   (Hebrews 12:1)

Thus, we have the complete picture. Jesus Christ has risen from the dead. He is a type of firstfruits. As a result of His resurrection, not only were there firstfruits on the day of His resurrection, but since then there have been many more firstfruits. All the true followers of Jesus Christ who have died, will rise again on that last day as firstfruits in Jesus Christ.

Those who are Christ's at His coming

When Christ returns for the second time, those believers who are still on the earth will rise to meet Him at His coming and those who are already dead will accompany Him on His return:

> *"But I do not want you to be ignorant, brethren, concerning those who have fallen asleep, lest you sorrow as others who have no hope. For if we believe that Jesus died and rose again, even so God will bring with Him those who sleep in Jesus. For this we say to you by the word of the Lord, that we who are alive and remain until the coming of the Lord will by no means precede those who are asleep. For the Lord Himself will descend from heaven with a shout, with the voice of an archangel, and with the trumpet of God. And the dead in Christ will rise first. Then we who are alive and remain shall be caught up together with them in the clouds to meet the Lord in the air. And thus we shall always be with the Lord. Therefore comfort one another with these words."*
>
> (1 Thessalonians 4:13–18)

The words "caught up" mean "taken suddenly or swiftly." As Peter says in his second letter, the day of the Lord will come like a thief in the night.

Points of view

There are several points of view in the body of Christ concerning the so-called "rapture." Some Christians believe that we will be taken up or raptured before the second coming of Christ and the tribulation. Others believe it will happen midway through the tribulation, and yet others at the end of the tribulation. Each of us must reach our own conclusion in this matter.

I, personally, take 1 Thessalonians 4 to be a confirmation of Matthew 24:30–31:

> *"For the Lord Himself will descend from heaven with a shout, with the voice of an archangel, and with the trumpet of God. And the dead in Christ will rise first."* (1 Thessalonians 4:16)

> *"Then the sign of the Son of Man will appear in heaven, and then all the tribes of the earth will mourn, and they will see the Son of Man coming on the clouds of heaven with power and great glory. And He will send His angels with a great sound of a*

trumpet, and they will gather together His elect from the four winds, from one end of heaven to the other."

(Matthew 24:30–31)

The events in this second scripture are described as having occurred after the great tribulation. If we put these two scriptures together, it would seem that Jesus Christ will not return for His elect until after that event.

However, each of us must be guided by the Holy Spirit on this matter.

We must always be ready

"But the day of the Lord will come as a thief in the night, in which the heavens will pass away with a great noise, and the elements will melt with fervent heat; both the earth and the works that are in it will be burned up."   (2 Peter 3:10)

Jesus Himself said in Revelation:

"Behold, I am coming as a thief. Blessed is he who watches, and keeps his garments, lest he walk naked and they see his shame."

(Revelation 16:15)

This is the same simile He had used while still on the earth:

"But know this, that if the master of the house had known what hour the thief would come, he would have watched and not allowed his house to be broken into."   (Matthew 24:43)

Twinkling of an eye

The Apostle Paul gives us further light on this mystery. He says that those who are followers of Jesus Christ at the time of His returning, will be changed in the twinkling of an eye:

"Now this I say, brethren, that flesh and blood cannot inherit the kingdom of God; nor does corruption inherit incorruption. Behold, I tell you a mystery: We shall not all sleep, but we shall all be changed – in a moment, in the twinkling of an eye, at the last trumpet. For the trumpet will sound, and the dead will be raised incorruptible, and we shall be changed. For this corruptible must put on incorruption, and this mortal must put on immortality."   (1 Corinthians 15:50–53)

Summary

1. Through Adam came spiritual death, but through Jesus Christ comes the resurrection of the dead.

2. Christ was the first to rise from the dead and is described as *"the firstfruit."*

3. The *"sheaf of the firstfruits"* is a type of Jesus Christ arising from the dead.

4. The waving of the firstfruits of the harvest was a triumphant act as well as an act of worship, confirming that the remaining harvest would be safely brought in.

5. Jesus spoke about a grain of wheat falling into the ground, dying and then producing much grain. In the same way, Jesus Christ had to fall to the ground and die, but by His resurrection from the dead He has fulfilled God's purposes and given us assurance of God's love in our lives.

6. At the time of the crucifixion of Jesus Christ, the bodies of many of the saints who had fallen asleep were raised.

7. Like a single grain of wheat falling into the ground, Jesus Christ died a lonely death, but when He arose from the dead He was no longer on His own but brought with Him the firstfruits of the resurrection.

8. Jesus Christ preached to the spirits in prison and proclaimed the good news of His death and coming resurrection to the righteous dead as well as to the disobedient.

9. Jesus ascended into heaven with the righteous dead who had been captives in Sheol.

10. On His final ascension into heaven, there was a cloud of His saints with Him.

11. Since that day there have been more firstfruits in the form of saints who have lived and died on this earth and gone into the presence of God.

12. When Jesus returns for the second time, those believers who are still on earth will rise to meet Him at His coming. He will bring with Him those who are already dead in Him.

13. We must always be ready for the return of Christ.

14. We shall all be changed in the twinkling of an eye.

Chapter 21

With What Body
Shall We Be Raised?

Paul deals with this question in his first letter to the Corinthians:

> "But someone will say, 'How are the dead raised up? And with what body do they come?' Foolish one, what you sow is not made alive unless it dies. And what you sow, you do not sow that body that shall be, but mere grain – perhaps wheat or some other grain. But God gives it a body as He pleases, and to each seed its own body. All flesh is not the same flesh, but there is one kind of flesh of men, another flesh of animals, another of fish, and another of birds. There are also celestial bodies and terrestrial bodies; but the glory of the celestial is one, and the glory of the terrestrial is another. There is one glory of the sun, another glory of the moon, and another glory of the stars; for one star differs from another star in glory."   (1 Corinthians 15:35–41)

Later he comments:

> "For this corruptible must put on incorruption, and this mortal must put on immortality."   (1 Corinthians 15:53)

Paul is saying that when we sow grain, a plant grows which does not resemble the grain. The original grain produces a new body but there still remains a direct relationship between the original seed and the new body. The type of body which is produced depends on the type of grain that is sown. From these comments we can conclude that there is a direct relationship between our earthly body and the spiritual body which we will be given on resurrection. There will be some obvious changes and the outward appearance and form of our new resurrected body will be different from the original body that was buried or cremated. However, from the scriptures already quoted from the Old Testament, it is clear that we will be able to recognize one another.

Paul's words make it equally clear that we will receive an incorruptible body, one which is immortal. Our present body of dishonor is called a *"lowly body"* in Philippians because it is the result of our sin and disobedience to God:

> *"who will transform our lowly body that it may be conformed to His glorious body, according to the working by which He is able even to subdue all things to Himself."*   (Philippians 3:21)

Our new resurrection body will be a transformed and glorious body, similar to that of Jesus. It will not be subject to the limits presently imposed upon it.

The grain of wheat

Paul makes the statement that what we sow does not come to life unless it dies. And, as we have seen, the seed of grain does not resemble the fully grown plant. As Jesus said:

> *"Most assuredly, I say to you, unless a grain of wheat falls into the ground and dies, it remains alone; but if it dies, it produces much grain."*   (John 12:24)

Unless the grain of wheat falls into the ground and dies, it produces nothing; but the seed that is allowed to die first produces a plant and then many ears of wheat.

Thus, God grants to each type of seed a plant or body of His choice.

As Paul explains, the flesh of human beings, animals, fish and birds all differ. Similarly, each of the heavenly bodies have differing brightness and content. Some stars are brighter than others, and the brightness of the sun is far greater than the brightness of the moon.

Natural body – spiritual body

Paul now compares our natural body with our spiritual body:

> *"So also is the resurrection of the dead. The body is sown in corruption, it is raised in incorruption. It is sown in dishonor, it is raised in glory. It is sown in weakness, it is raised in power. It is sown a natural body, it is raised a spiritual body. There is a natural body, and there is a spiritual body. And so it is written, 'The first man Adam became a living being.' The last Adam became a life-giving spirit."* (1 Corinthians 15:42–45)

Orders of glory

Even among the resurrected believers, there will be different orders of glory:

> *"And many of those who sleep in the dust of the earth shall awake,*
> *Some to everlasting life,*
> *Some to shame and everlasting contempt.*
> *Those who are wise shall shine*
> *Like the brightness of the firmament,*
> *And those who turn many to righteousness*
> *Like the stars forever and ever."* (Daniel 12:2–3)

Thus, those who proclaim the word of God and encourage others to turn to Jesus Christ will be like the stars shining brightly forever and ever.

Reforming of our body

God's foreknowledge of us in every way is discussed in Psalm 139:

> *"For You formed my inward parts;*
> *You covered me in my mother's womb.*
> *I will praise You, for I am fearfully and wonderfully made;*
> *Marvelous are Your works,*
> *And that my soul knows very well.*
> *My frame was not hidden from You,*
> *When I was made in secret,*
> *And skillfully wrought in the lowest parts of the earth.*
> *Your eyes saw my substance, being yet unformed.*
> *And in Your book they all were written,*
> *The days fashioned for me,*
> *When as yet there were none of them."* (Psalm 139:13–16)

God knows every part of our being and even saw us before our physical bodies were formed. Even though a body may have been in the grave for many years or may have been cremated God is able to reform it into a spiritual body. With God nothing will be impossible.

The resurrected body of Jesus

When He appeared to His disciples following His resurrection, Jesus gave specific proof of the fact that He was in His resurrected body. This body had physical attributes similar to a normal body. It needed to be real enough to convince doubting Thomas who had said:

> *"Unless I see in His hands the print of the nails, and put my finger into the print of the nails, and put my hand into His side, I will not believe."* (John 20:25)

Eight days later when Jesus stood in the midst of His disciples once again, He invited Thomas to reach out and touch Him:

> *"Then He said to Thomas, 'Reach your finger here, and look at My hands; and reach your hand here, and put it into My side. Do not be unbelieving, but believing.'"* (John 20:27)

Flesh and bones

Luke gives us a further description of Jesus' resurrection appearance. He says that the disciples were terrified and frightened when Jesus appeared to them and supposed they had seen a spirit. Then we read:

> *"And He said to them, 'Why are you troubled? And why do doubts arise in your hearts? Behold My hands and My feet, that it is I Myself. Handle Me and see, for a spirit does not have flesh and bones as you see I have.' When He had said this, He showed them His hands and His feet."* (Luke 24:38–40)

After this Jesus asked for food and they gave him a piece of broiled fish and some honeycomb which He took and ate in their presence.

Nevertheless, despite the fact that His body had the attributes and appearances of a normal physical body, we note that He could appear and disappear at will:

> *"Now it came to pass, as He sat at the table with them, that He took bread, blessed and broke it, and gave it to them. Then their eyes were opened and they knew Him; and He vanished from their sight."*   (Luke 24:30–31)

First ascension of Jesus

Apart from appearing and disappearing at will, the resurrected Jesus Christ could ascend into heaven and return to earth. Under the old covenant, the High Priest could not be touched by anybody when he went into the Holy of Holies, otherwise that person would die. Similarly, when Jesus appeared to Mary immediately after His resurrection, He had yet to take His blood and present it in heaven, and that is why He said to Mary:

> *"Do not cling to Me, for I have not yet ascended to My Father; but go to My brethren and say to them, 'I am ascending to My Father and your Father, and to My God and your God.'"*
> (John 20:17)

After that ascension He returned to earth and appeared to His disciples for forty days.

The believer's new body

The believer is promised a similar body to that of Christ:

> *"As was the man of dust, so also are those who are made of dust; and as is the heavenly Man, so also are those who are heavenly. And as we have borne the image of the man of dust, we shall also bear the image of the heavenly Man."*
> (1 Corinthians 15:48–49)

In the same way as the first man, Adam, was a *"man of dust"* and we are people of dust, so those of us who will be with Jesus Christ will be transformed to bear His image. This is further confirmed in Paul's letter to the Philippians:

> *"For our citizenship is in heaven, from which we also eagerly wait for the Savior, the Lord Jesus Christ, who will transform our lowly body that it may be conformed to His glorious body, according to the working by which He is able even to subdue all things to Himself."*   (Philippians 3:20–21)

Here we are promised that our present body will be transformed into a glorious body which is like that of the resurrected Lord Jesus Christ.

Relationships

The Gospels record a conversation which Jesus had with some Sadducees on the subject of the resurrection of the dead. The Sadducees, who said there was no resurrection, quoted a case of seven brothers, all of whom in turn married the same widow and in turn died, but no children were produced. It was the custom under the law for the brother to marry the widow of a deceased brother if there were no children, so that children could be born who could carry on the dead man's family line. The Sadducees asked Jesus whose wife this woman would be in the resurrection.

In response Jesus Christ then made a most interesting statement:

> *"You are mistaken, not knowing the Scriptures nor the power of God. For in the resurrection they neither marry nor are given in marriage, but are like angels of God in heaven."*
>
> (Matthew 22:29–30)

His words clearly indicate that marriages do not continue in heaven. In resurrection we will be like the angels of God.

Then Jesus Christ went on to say that Abraham, Isaac and Jacob were not dead but alive because they had eternal life. In this way, He absolutely contradicted the understanding of the Sadducees, who denied there was any resurrection:

> *"'I am the God of Abraham, the God of Isaac, and the God of Jacob'? God is not the God of the dead, but of the living."*
>
> (Matthew 22:32)

We accordingly have a very clear statement from Jesus that there is a resurrection of the dead.

Unrighteous dead

Jesus spoke of two resurrections: the resurrection of life and the resurrection of condemnation. Jesus spoke of a time when all who were in the grave would hear His voice:

"and come forth – those who have done good, to the resurrection of life, and those who have done evil, to the resurrection of condemnation."   (John 5:29)

Scripture does not appear to give any indication about the form of body the unrighteous dead will have.

Anti-Christ

The debate about the resurrection of the body continued on into the first century. John raises the issue in his first letter, pointing out that many anti-Christs, who had previously belonged to the church, had gone out from the church. These people were denying the resurrection of Jesus Christ and that He is the Messiah:

"They went out from us, but they were not of us; for if they had been of us, they would have continued with us; but they went out that they might be made manifest, that none of them were of us."   (1 John 2:19)

"Who is a liar but he who denies that Jesus is the Christ? He is antichrist who denies the Father and the Son. Whoever denies the Son does not have the Father either; he who acknowledges the Son has the Father also."   (1 John 2:22–23)

Unless such people repent, their eternal destiny will be among the unrighteous dead.

The two resurrections

We also read of two resurrections in the book of Revelation. John was given a vision of the souls of those who had been beheaded for their witness to Jesus and His word, and who had not worshipped the beast or his image and had not received his mark on their foreheads or their hands. These martyrs will be brought to life in the first resurrection, and will live and reign with Jesus Christ for a thousand years. They will be priests of God and of Christ.

The rest of the dead will not live again until the thousand years are finished:

"And I saw thrones, and they sat on them, and judgment was committed to them. Then I saw the souls of those who had been

beheaded for their witness to Jesus and for the word of God, who had not worshipped the beast or his image, and had not received his mark on their foreheads or on their hands. And they lived and reigned with Christ for a thousand years. But the rest of the dead did not live again until the thousand years were finished. This is the first resurrection. Blessed and holy is he who has part in the first resurrection. Over such the second death has no power, but they shall be priests of God and of Christ, and shall reign with Him a thousand years."   (Revelation 20:4–6)

Those who participate in the first resurrection do not have to worry about the second death because it has no power over them. The second death will be reserved for those who are condemned for eternity and are cast into the lake of fire.

"And anyone not found written in the Book of Life was cast into the lake of fire."   (Revelation 20:15)

Believers take part in first resurrection

Jesus has promised us:

"Most assuredly, I say to you, he who hears My word and believes in Him who sent Me has everlasting life, and shall not come into judgment, but has passed from death into life."

(John 5:24)

Those who are the true followers of Jesus Christ can expect to take part in the first resurrection. We will have more to say about this when we look at the question of eternal judgment.

Summary

1. When we sow grain, a plant grows which does not resemble the original grain.

2. There is a direct relationship between the original seed and the new body.

3. The type of plant produced depends on the type of grain sown.

4. We can conclude that there is a direct relationship between our earthly body and the spiritual body which we will be given on resurrection.

5. We will be able to recognize one another.

6. Our present body is a *"lowly body,"* but our new resurrection body will be beautiful and glorious, not subject to the limitations presently imposed upon us.

7. There is a natural body and a spiritual body.

8. There are orders of glory.

9. God knows every part of our being and saw us even before our physical bodies were formed. God is able to reform the dead body even though it has been in the grave or cremated for many years so that it becomes a spiritual body.

10. Jesus' resurrected body had physical attributes similar to those of a normal body.

11. When Jesus first appeared to Mary Magdalene, she was not able to touch Him because, like the High Priest, He had to go into the presence of God.

12. The believer is promised a similar body to that of Jesus Christ.

13. Relationships such as marriage will not continue in heaven.

14. There are two resurrections, one for the righteous dead and one for the unrighteous.

15. Those who take part in the first resurrection will live and reign with Jesus Christ for a thousand years. The rest of the dead will not be raised until the end of that time.

Chapter 22

Resurrection Life Now

Jesus gives us resurrection life now

Lazarus of Bethany had died. He had been dead and in the tomb for four days.

Jesus had not hurried to get back to Bethany. Now He had arrived and Martha went out to meet Him saying,

> "Lord, if You had been here, my brother would not have died. But even now I know that whatever You ask of God, God will give You." (John 11:21–22)

Then Jesus made a statement of tremendous moment. He said to Martha, *"Your brother will rise again."* Martha responded that she was well aware that her brother would rise again in the resurrection at the last day. She believed in that resurrection.

However, Jesus said to her:

> "I am the resurrection and the life. He who believes in Me, though he may die, he shall live. And whoever lives and believes in Me shall never die. Do you believe this?" (John 11:25–26)

Yes, it is through Jesus Christ that we can have resurrection life now. When we are born again and receive the Holy Spirit, the presence of Jesus enters us as He gives us eternal life.

Man became a living being

When God formed Adam out of the dust of the ground, He breathed into his nostrils the breath of life and Adam became a living being:

> *"And the* Lord *God formed man of the dust of the ground, and breathed into his nostrils the breath of life; and man became a living being."*   (Genesis 2:7)

Jesus became a life-giving spirit

Jesus Christ is described in the Bible as the last Adam. Through resurrection He became a life-giving spirit:

> *"And so it is written, 'The first man Adam became a living being.' The last Adam became a life-giving spirit."*
>   (1 Corinthians 15:45)

When God formed Adam from the dust of the ground and breathed into his nostrils, Adam came alive as a human being. However, when Jesus Christ rose from the dead, He became a life-giving spirit. He breathed on His disciples and they received the Holy Spirit. Thus they were born again.

> *"And when He had said this, He breathed on them, and said to them, 'Receive the Holy Spirit.' "*   (John 20:22)

When we turn to Jesus Christ and are born again, we receive the Holy Spirit. Jesus becomes a life-giving spirit to each of us. In this way we obtain resurrection life.

The spiritually dead

On this earth, before His death and resurrection, Jesus Christ proclaimed that the righteous dead would hear His voice and that they would live forever:

> *"Most assuredly, I say to you, the hour is coming, and now is, when the dead will hear the voice of the Son of God; and those who hear will live."*   (John 5:25)

This, of course, is referring to those people who, when they hear the gospel of Jesus Christ, respond and are born again. They are no longer spiritually dead but are made alive through Jesus Christ.

Our coming to the heavenly Jerusalem

In one sense already we have come into the presence of the

righteous dead as we have committed our lives to the lordship of Jesus Christ:

> *"But you have come to Mount Zion and to the city of the living God, the heavenly Jerusalem, to an innumerable company of angels, to the general assembly and church of the firstborn who are registered in heaven, to God the Judge of all, to the spirits of just men made perfect, to Jesus the Mediator of the new covenant, and to the blood of sprinkling that speaks better things than that of Abel."* (Hebrews 12:22–24)

As we commence our Christian walk, we realize that God is with us by His Holy Spirit. His presence becomes ever stronger as we obey Him. It is then that we begin to understand spiritual things and have a realization that we can come into His presence as we wait upon Him. We are often aware of the presence of angels and of Jesus Himself.

Throne of grace

When we are born again, we can, in the Spirit, come boldly to the throne of grace and into the presence of God through Jesus Christ Himself.

> *"Therefore, brethren, having boldness to enter the Holiest by the blood of Jesus, by a new and living way which He consecrated for us, through the veil, that is, His flesh, and having a High Priest over the house of God ... "* (Hebrews 10:19–21)

We can therefore believe that we are already in the presence of God Himself and we should have the love, joy and peace of God in our hearts.

Summary

1. Jesus Christ is the resurrection and life eternal.

2. When God formed Adam out of the dust of the ground, He breathed into his nostrils the breath of life and Adam became a living being.

3. Jesus Christ is the last Adam; He became a life-giving spirit.

4. Jesus Christ is the life-giving spirit who breathes upon us that we may receive the gift of eternal life.

5. By committing our lives to the lordship of Jesus Christ we have already come into the presence of the righteous dead.

6. Because Jesus Christ is the Mediator of the new covenant, we can come boldly to the throne of grace and into the presence of God through Jesus Christ Himself.

Chapter 23

Eternal Judgment

God the Judge

One of the most striking aspects of the Old Testament is the revelation of the nature of God Himself. He chose His special people, Israel, and manifested His mighty power to them by taking them through the Red Sea. He went before them in a cloud by day and in a pillar of fire by night. He revealed Himself in many ways to them and often saved them from their enemies. Despite the fact that they continuously rebelled against Him, His mercy never failed. As the psalmist says in Psalm 136:

> *"Oh, give thanks to the LORD, for He is good!*
> *For His mercy endures forever.*
> *Oh, give thanks to the God of gods!*
> *For His mercy endures forever.*
> *Oh, give thanks to the Lord of lords!*
> *For His mercy endures forever:*
> *To Him who alone does great wonders,*
> *For His mercy endures forever;*
> *To Him who by wisdom made the heavens,*
> *For His mercy endures forever;*
> *To Him who laid out the earth above the waters,*
> *For His mercy endures forever;*
> *To Him who made great lights,*
> *For His mercy endures forever–*
> *The sun to rule by day,*
> *For His mercy endures forever;*
> *The moon and stars to rule by night,*
> *For His mercy endures forever."*   (Psalm 136:1–9)

God is long-suffering and merciful

> *"And the* LORD *passed before him and proclaimed, 'The* LORD, *the* LORD *God, merciful and gracious, longsuffering, and abounding in goodness and truth.'"*   (Exodus 34:6)

The judgment of God

Scripture makes it very clear that we live only once on this earth. There is no such thing as reincarnation. This is a doctrine of Hinduism which has no relevance or truth before God. Thus, we find from Scripture:

> *"And as it is appointed for men to die once, but after this the judgment ..."*   (Hebrews 9:27)

Thus, all of us must die once, and after that we must face the judgment of God.

Rebellion of Israel

Despite all His goodness toward them, the Israelites sorely tried the Lord's patience by their rebellion. The psalmist sets it out as follows:

> *"Nevertheless they flattered Him with their mouth,*
> *And they lied to Him with their tongue;*
> *For their heart was not steadfast with Him,*
> *Nor were they faithful in His covenant.*
> *But He, being full of compassion, forgave their iniquity,*
> *And did not destroy them.*
> *Yes, many a time He turned His anger away,*
> *And did not stir up all His wrath;*
> *For He remembered that they were but flesh,*
> *A breath that passes away and does not come again."*
>   (Psalm 78:36–39)

The revelation of Scripture is that God is just, merciful, compassionate and long-suffering.

Judge of all the earth

It is clear that God is Judge of all the earth:

> *"Far be it from You to do such a thing as this, to slay the*
> *righteous with the wicked, so that the righteous should be as the*
> *wicked; far be it from You! Shall not the Judge of all the earth do*
> *right?"* (Genesis 18:25)

This is confirmed in Psalm 94:

> *"Rise up, O Judge of the earth;*
> *Render punishment to the proud."* (Psalm 94:2)

God is sovereign and is the final Judge of all:

> *"So that men will say,*
> *'Surely there is a reward for the righteous;*
> *Surely He is God who judges in the earth.'"* (Psalm 58:11)

God shall judge the world in righteousness

> *"He shall judge the world in righteousness,*
> *And He shall administer judgment for the peoples in*
> *uprightness."* (Psalm 9:8)

God is not only Judge of all the earth, but His nature is to be
compassionate and longsuffering and His judgment will be in
righteousness.

New Testament

The New Testament confirms the sovereignty of God as Judge:

> *"And if you call on the Father, who without partiality judges*
> *according to each one's work, conduct yourselves throughout the*
> *time of your stay here in fear."* (1 Peter 1:17)

But it also reveals that He is a merciful and longsuffering God:

> *"For God did not send His Son into the world to condemn the*
> *world, but that the world through Him might be saved."*
> (John 3:17)

> *"The Lord is not slack concerning His promise, as some count*
> *slackness, but is longsuffering toward us, not willing that any*
> *should perish but that all should come to repentance."*
> (2 Peter 3:9)

Jesus as the Judge of the world

Although God is Judge of all the earth, He has committed all judgment to the Son:

> *"For the Father judges no one, but has committed all judgment to the Son, that all should honour the Son just as they honor the Father. He who does not honor the Son does not honour the Father who sent Him."* (John 5:22–23)

Revelation 19 pictures Jesus as the Judge of the world seated on His white horse:

> *"Now I saw heaven opened, and behold, a white horse. And He who sat on him was called Faithful and True, and in righteousness He judges and makes war."* (Revelation 19:11)

Jesus came into this world for judgment:

> *"And Jesus said, 'For judgment I have come into this world, that those who do not see may see, and that those who see may be made blind.'"* (John 9:39)

Jesus exercises authority

Because Jesus is the Son of Man and shared the experience of human beings by becoming one of us, He is fully aware of our weaknesses and of our troubles. This is the reason why God has given Him authority to carry out judgment:

> *"and has given Him authority to execute judgment also, because He is the Son of Man."* (John 5:27)

> *"He who rejects Me, and does not receive My words, has that which judges him – the word that I have spoken will judge him in the last day."* (John 12:48)

The final authority for judgment is vested in Jesus Christ by God Himself, a fact which Paul explained in the sermon he preached in Athens:

> *"because He has appointed a day on which He will judge the world in righteousness by the Man whom He has ordained. He has given assurance of this to all by raising Him from the dead."* (Acts 17:31)

Paul makes another reference to Jesus as the Judge in his second letter to Timothy. He exhorts Timothy:

> *"I charge you therefore before God and the Lord Jesus Christ, who will judge the living and the dead at His appearing and His kingdom."* (2 Timothy 4:1)

Peter also warns of the judgment that awaits those who are not willing to listen to the Lord:

> *"They will give an account to Him who is ready to judge the living and the dead ... "* (1 Peter 4:5)

Words of Jesus will judge us

Even though He has been given authority to judge, Jesus makes this interesting statement regarding judgment:

> *"And if anyone hears My words and does not believe, I do not judge him; for I did not come to judge the world but to save the world."* (John 12:47)

Jesus did not come to judge the world but to save it. It will be His words that judge us:

> *"He who rejects Me, and does not receive My words, has that which judges him – the word that I have spoken will judge him in the last day."* (John 12:48)

Even though Jesus Christ has received authority from God to judge, we now find that, in His mercy, He has set out how we shall be judged. It will be the words which Jesus has spoken that will judge us in the last day. Hence, we need to take very careful note of the word of God.

Judging ourselves

Scripture tells us that we can avoid judgment by judging ourselves. We can judge ourselves by the words of Jesus:

> *"For if we would judge ourselves, we would not be judged."* (1 Corinthians 11:31)

Paul is speaking in the context of those who eat the bread and drink the cup of the Lord in an unworthy manner. He explains that individuals should examine themselves before taking communion, so that they do not bring judgment on themselves. If we are living in a sinful situation and do not repent before coming to the place of communion, then we are in danger of drinking judgment upon ourselves.

Daniel's vision

The Old Testament prophets all had a clear understanding that there would be a Day of Judgment, and Daniel was no exception. God gave him a tremendous vision of that Day:

> *"I watched till thrones were put in place,*
> *And the Ancient of Days was seated;*
> *His garment was white as snow,*
> *And the hair of His head was like pure wool.*
> *His throne was a fiery flame,*
> *Its wheels a burning fire;*
> *A fiery stream issued*
> *And came forth from before Him.*
> *A thousand thousands ministered to Him;*
> *Ten thousand times ten thousand stood before Him.*
> *The court was seated,*
> *And the books were opened."*   (Daniel 7:9–10)

How God judges

Four important principles of God's judgment are set out in Romans 2.

1. God's judgment is according to truth

> *"Therefore you are inexcusable, O man, whoever you are who judge, for in whatever you judge another you condemn yourself; for you who judge practice the same things. But we know that the judgment of God is according to truth against those who practice such things."*   (Romans 2:1–2)

God's judgment is with absolute truth. Jesus Christ is the way, the truth and the life and God Himself embraces all truth.

Whenever we judge another, we should apply the same standard of judgment to ourselves. The above scripture is referring to religious people who judge others, yet themselves are doing the same wrong things. God is aware of everything in our heart and mind and will judge us accordingly.

2. It is according to our deeds

"who 'will render to each one according to his deeds.'"

(Romans 2:6)

This is further confirmed in Revelation 20:12:

"And I saw the dead, small and great, standing before God, and books were opened. And another book was opened, which is the Book of Life. And the dead were judged according to their works, by the things which were written in the books."

(Revelation 20:12)

3. God is not partial

"For there is no partiality with God."   (Romans 2:11)

It doesn't matter who we are, God is no respecter of persons.

4. Judged by our revelation of God

The next principle of God's judgment is set out in Romans 2:12:

"For as many as have sinned without law will also perish without law, and as many as have sinned in the law will be judged by the law ..."

Those who have heard the gospel of Jesus Christ will be judged by it. Those who have a full knowledge of God's laws and standards will be judged according to those laws, but those who do not know the law of Moses will be judged in accordance with the general understanding of God which has been granted to the human race as a whole as they look at creation.

Thus, summing up, there are four main principles of God's judgment:

1. it is according to truth;
2. it is according to our deeds or works;
3. it is without respect of persons;
4. it is according to the light we have received.

The wrath of God

Scripture tells us it is a fearful thing to fall into the hands of the living God.

Those who have received a knowledge of the truth but nevertheless deliberately sin, must certainly expect to face God's judgment:

> *"For if we sin willfully after we have received the knowledge of the truth, there no longer remains a sacrifice for sins, but a certain fearful expectation of judgment, and fiery indignation which will devour the adversaries. Anyone who has rejected Moses' law dies without mercy on the testimony of two or three witnesses. Of how much worse punishment, do you suppose, will he be thought worthy who has trampled the Son of God underfoot, counted the blood of the covenant by which he was sanctified a common thing, and insulted the Spirit of grace? For we know Him who said, 'Vengeance is Mine, I will repay,' says the Lord. And again, 'The Lord will judge His people.' It is a fearful thing to fall into the hands of the living God."*
>
> (Hebrews 10:26–31)

This scripture refers to continued deliberate and willful sin.

The pardon of God

On the cross Jesus Christ has carried our sins and iniquities and has pardoned our sins. Therefore, when we turn to Him in true repentance, we are delivered from the power of sin and from God's wrath. Then, once again, God offers us reconciliation through Jesus Christ:

> *"If we confess our sins, He is faithful and just to forgive us our sins and to cleanse us from all unrighteousness."*
>
> (1 John 1:9)

The mercy of God is from everlasting to everlasting. If we do sin deliberately, but then come back into true repentance before God, it is clear that His mercy prevails.

However, if we continue to sin willfully after we have received the knowledge of the truth, then we come under God's judgment. It would be a terrible thing to die while willfully sinning.

Conclusion

God is a merciful, righteous Judge who, Himself, has committed all judgment to Jesus Christ. Jesus has told us that His words will judge us. For those who seek to obey God, His mercy and justice will prevail. Those who deliberately disobey on a continuous basis will face the wrath of God. Scripture tells us that if we will judge ourselves, we will not be judged. Throughout all of this, we see the ever-loving hand of God extended out to all of humankind. The Lord is not willing that any should perish, but wants all to come to repentance. God's pardon is freely available to all who turn to Him.

Summary

1. God is the eternal Judge.
2. God is longsuffering and merciful.
3. All human beings will face God's judgment.
4. Despite the goodness of God toward them, the Israelites rebelled.
5. God is Judge of all the earth.
6. The Lord shall judge the world in righteousness.
7. God is sovereign but He has committed all judgment to His Son Jesus Christ.
8. His words will judge us.
9. If we will judge ourselves, we will not be judged.
10. Daniel had a vision of the Day of Judgment.
11. God's judgment is according to truth.
12. It is according to our deeds.
13. God is not partial in His judgment.
14. It is according to the light we have received.
15. It is a fearful thing to fall into the hands of the living God and we should avoid God's wrath at all costs by obeying Him.
16. God offers us His pardon through Jesus Christ.

Chapter 24

Judgment for the Christian

In John's Gospel, Jesus Christ offers tremendous reassurance to the committed Christian. He specifically points out that those who hear His word and believe in Him shall have everlasting life and shall not come into judgment:

> *"Most assuredly, I say to you, he who hears My word and believes in Him who sent Me has everlasting life, and shall not come into judgment, but has passed from death into life."*
>
> (John 5:24)

The word "believe" here means to "put trust in," "commit oneself to." If we do truly place our trust in Jesus Christ, commit ourselves to Him and listen to His word, then we will obey Him. If we obey Him, then we are assured of eternal life.

No condemnation

Scripture gives us this promise:

> *"There is therefore now no condemnation to those who are in Christ Jesus, who do not walk according to the flesh, but according to the Spirit. For the law of the Spirit of life in Christ Jesus has made me free from the law of sin and death."*
>
> (Romans 8:1–2)

True followers of Jesus Christ have been made righteous through Him and therefore will not be judged according to the requirements of the law. As we set our minds on the things of the Spirit and not the things of the flesh, then we are following and obeying Jesus Christ.

True followers of Jesus Christ

It is clear that those believers in Jesus Christ who trust Him and obey Him while they live on this earth, are part of God's elect. Jesus says this about them:

> *"My sheep hear My voice, and I know them, and they follow Me. And I give them eternal life, and they shall never perish; neither shall anyone snatch them out of My hand. My Father, who has given them to Me, is greater than all; and no one is able to snatch them out of My Father's hand. I and My Father are one."*
> (John 10:27–30)

This is confirmed in John 8:

> *"Most assuredly, I say to you, if anyone keeps My word he shall never see death."* (John 8:51)

The death that Jesus Christ is referring to here, of course, is spiritual death, that is separation from God. Those who remain faithful to the Lord during this lifetime will never undergo spiritual death and separation from God.

This is also confirmed in John 5:24:

> *"Most assuredly, I say to you, he who hears My word and believes in Him who sent Me has everlasting life, and shall not come into judgment, but has passed from death into life."*

Therefore, those who are true sheep of Jesus Christ, having remained true to His word and obeyed Him, will enter eternal life.

The first resurrection

Revelation 20:6 says:

> *"Blessed and holy is he who has part in the first resurrection. Over such the second death has no power, but they shall be priests of God and of Christ, and shall reign with Him a thousand years."*

These holy ones will share in Christ's reign:

> *"And I saw thrones, and they sat on them, and judgment was committed to them. Then I saw the souls of those who had been beheaded for their witness to Jesus and for the word of God, who had not worshipped the beast or his image, and had not received*

*his mark on their foreheads or on their hands. And they lived
and reigned with Christ for a thousand years."*

(Revelation 20:4)

Among those who take part in the first resurrection will be the
faithful servants of Christ who have been granted resurrection
to eternal life. In addition, there will be the righteous dead who,
until the time of Jesus' resurrection, had been in that part of
Sheol known as "Abraham's bosom" (see also pp. 139–140.):

"Therefore He says:

*'When He ascended on high,
He led captivity captive,
And gave gifts to men.'"*

(Ephesians 4:8)

After proclaiming the good news to them, He then took them
with Him into heaven.

*"For this reason the gospel was preached also to those who are
dead, that they might be judged according to men in the flesh,
but live according to God in the spirit."*

(1 Peter 4:6)

Those who live in true obedience to Jesus Christ, having carried
out His commandments and His works, have been given the
Holy Spirit as a guarantee:

*"Now He who has prepared us for this very thing is God, who
also has given us the Spirit as a guarantee."*

(2 Corinthians 5:5)

Paul looks to the first resurrection

Paul looked forward, with confidence, to the first resurrection:

*"So we are always confident, knowing that while we are at home
in the body we are absent from the Lord. For we walk by faith,
not by sight. We are confident, yes, well pleased rather to be
absent from the body and to be present with the Lord."*

(2 Corinthians 5:6–8)

Those who are alive at the return of Jesus Christ

Those who are alive on this earth when Jesus Christ returns and
who are true believers in Him, will be caught up in the air to
meet Him:

"For the Lord Himself will descend from heaven with a shout, with the voice of an archangel, and with the trumpet of God. And the dead in Christ will rise first. Then we who are alive and remain shall be caught up together with them in the clouds to meet the Lord in the air. And thus we shall always be with the Lord." (1 Thessalonians 4:16–17)

Crown of righteousness

We should all walk in the same confidence as Paul did, knowing that, as we are truly obedient to the Lord Jesus Christ and follow His commands, then there is a crown of righteousness laid up for us:

"I have fought the good fight, I have finished the race, I have kept the faith. Finally, there is laid up for me the crown of righteousness, which the Lord, the righteous Judge, will give to me on that Day, and not to me only but also to all who have loved His appearing." (2 Timothy 4:7–8)

When Jesus was asked by the people, what should they do in order to *"work the works of God,"* He answered:

"Jesus answered and said to them, 'This is the work of God, that you believe in Him whom He sent.'" (John 6:29)

Believing in Jesus Christ is obeying Him, proclaiming the good news of the gospel to the very ends of the earth and carrying out His works, including taking care of the poor, the sick, the thirsty, the naked, the stranger, the hungry and those in prison. It means living in true holiness before God and deliberately turning away from sin. We have all been given talents to use in our service of God, and, if we fail to do so, then we will become an unprofitable servant who will be cast into darkness. Our fate will have already been sealed before we leave this earth.

For the true followers of Jesus Christ, their appearance before the judgment seat of Christ will be an occasion not for condemnation but for reward. This reward will be based upon our works which, in turn, are based upon our faith in Jesus Christ who grants us His righteousness.

Summary

1. To believe in Jesus Christ means to put our trust in Him and commit ourselves to Him.

2. There is no condemnation for those who are in Christ Jesus and walk, not according to the flesh, but according to the Spirit.

3. Those believers in Jesus Christ who trust Him and obey Him while they live on this earth are part of God's elect.

4. Those who are alive at the time of the return of Jesus Christ will be caught up together with the risen dead to meet Him in the air.

5. Those who remain faithful to the Lord during this lifetime will never undergo spiritual death and separation from God.

6. Those who take part in the first resurrection will be priests of God and of Christ and will reign with Him for one thousand years.

7. Paul looked forward, with confidence, to the first resurrection.

8. Paul looked forward to receiving the crown of righteousness which every true believer will receive.

Chapter 25

Warnings for the Christian

Judgment seat of Christ

The word of God makes it clear that one day we shall all stand before the judgment seat of Christ. When Paul speaks about the "judgment seat," he uses the Greek word *bema*, which means "a raised platform."

If we have truly followed the Lord and obeyed Him, we have nothing to fear. However, Paul gives us the clear warning that every one of us will be required to give an account of ourselves to God:

> *"But why do you judge your brother? Or why do you show contempt for your brother? For we shall all stand before the judgment seat of Christ. For it is written:*
>
> *'As I live, says the* LORD,
> *Every knee shall bow to Me,*
> *And every tongue shall confess to God.'*
>
> *So then each of us shall give account of himself to God."*
>
> (Romans 14:10–12)

The word of God also tells us that one day all the secrets of our heart will be brought to the light:

> *"in the day when God will judge the secrets of men by Jesus Christ, according to my gospel."*   (Romans 2:16)

Jesus Christ has paid the full penalty for our sins, and if we have truly obeyed and followed Him, we will be blessed. If we do fall into sin, John assures us that we can come back to God:

> *"If we confess our sins, He is faithful and just to forgive us our sins and to cleanse us from all unrighteousness."*   (1 John 1:9)

Peter warns us

Peter also reinforces the fact that judgment will begin at the house of God:

> *"For the time has come for judgment to begin at the house of God; and if it begins with us first, what will be the end of those who do not obey the gospel of God? Now*
>
> *'If the righteous one is scarcely saved,*
> *Where will the ungodly and the sinner appear?'"*
>
> (1 Peter 4:17–18)

In his reference to the *"righteous one"* Peter is making it clear that, although we are made righteous through the death and resurrection of Jesus Christ by believing in Him, we are called to follow Him and obey Him, walking in the Spirit and not in the flesh.

Paul also refers to the judgment seat of Christ in his second letter to the Corinthians:

> *"Therefore we make it our aim, whether present or absent, to be well pleasing to Him. For we must all appear before the judgment seat of Christ, that each one may receive the things done in the body, according to what he has done, whether good or bad. Knowing, therefore, the terror of the Lord, we persuade men; but we are well known to God, and I also trust are well known in your consciences."* (2 Corinthians 5:9–11)

Here we see that we should always make it our aim to be well pleasing to God through Jesus Christ. We are clearly told that each one of us will be rewarded according to the things we have done while here on earth, whether good or bad.

Judgment according to obedience

There will be many who claim to be followers of Jesus Christ but whom He will disown on the last day:

> *"Not everyone who says to Me, 'Lord, Lord,' shall enter the kingdom of heaven, but he who does the will of My Father in heaven. Many will say to Me in that day, 'Lord, Lord, have we not prophesied in Your name, cast out demons in Your name, and done many wonders in Your name?' And then I will declare*

to them, *'I never knew you; depart from Me, you who practice lawlessness!'* " (Matthew 7:21–23)

It is the person who does the will of His Father in heaven who shall enter the kingdom of God. We shall be known by the fruits of our life:

"Even so, every good tree bears good fruit, but a bad tree bears bad fruit. A good tree cannot bear bad fruit, nor can a bad tree bear good fruit. Every tree that does not bear good fruit is cut down and thrown into the fire. Therefore by their fruits you will know them." (Matthew 7:17–20)

In the parable of the wise and foolish virgins, we have a clear lesson about the need to be ready at all times:

"Then the kingdom of heaven shall be likened to ten virgins who took their lamps and went out to meet the bridegroom. Now five of them were wise, and five were foolish. Those who were foolish took their lamps and took no oil with them, but the wise took oil in their vessels with their lamps. But while the bridegroom was delayed, they all slumbered and slept. And at midnight a cry was heard: 'Behold, the bridegroom is coming; go out to meet him!' Then all those virgins arose and trimmed their lamps. And the foolish said to the wise, 'Give us some of your oil, for our lamps are going out.' But the wise answered, saying, 'No, lest there should not be enough for us and you; but go rather to those who sell, and buy for yourselves.' And while they went to buy, the bridegroom came, and those who were ready went in with him to the wedding; and the door was shut. Afterward the other virgins came also, saying, 'Lord, Lord, open to us!' But he answered and said, 'Assuredly, I say to you, I do not know you.' Watch therefore, for you know neither the day nor the hour in which the Son of Man is coming." (Matthew 25:1–13)

Jesus is the vine

Jesus compared Himself to the vine, with ourselves as the branches. If we are living in Jesus Christ and obeying Him, then we will bear much fruit and will be pleasing to God the Father:

"Abide in Me, and I in you. As the branch cannot bear fruit of itself, unless it abides in the vine, neither can you, unless you abide in Me. I am the vine, you are the branches. He who abides

in Me, and I in him, bears much fruit; for without Me you can do nothing. If anyone does not abide in Me, he is cast out as a branch and is withered; and they gather them and throw them into the fire, and they are burned. If you abide in Me, and My words abide in you, you will ask what you desire, and it shall be done for you. By this My Father is glorified, that you bear much fruit; so you will be My disciples." (John 15:4–8)

Holiness needed

Just as the Israelites drank from the spiritual rock Jesus Christ (1 Corinthians 10:4), so we, as Christians, are given the privilege of drinking from the Holy Spirit. Each of the writers of the New Testament places heavy emphasis on the need for holiness in our walk with God. For example, we have already pointed out those who are excluded from the kingdom of God, as set out in Galatians 5:19–21:

"Now the works of the flesh are evident, which are: adultery, fornication, uncleanness, lewdness, idolatry, sorcery, hatred, contentions, jealousies, outbursts of wrath, selfish ambitions, dissensions, heresies, envy, murders, drunkenness, revelries, and the like; of which I tell you beforehand, just as I also told you in time past, that those who practice such things will not inherit the kingdom of God."

He reiterates this conviction both in his first letter to the Corinthians and in his letter to the Ephesians:

"Do you not know that the unrighteous will not inherit the kingdom of God? Do not be deceived. Neither fornicators, nor idolaters, nor adulterers, nor homosexuals, nor sodomites, nor thieves, nor covetous, nor drunkards, nor revilers, nor extortioners will inherit the kingdom of God." (1 Corinthians 6:9–10)

"And walk in love, as Christ also has loved us and given Himself for us, an offering and a sacrifice to God for a sweet-smelling aroma. But fornication and all uncleanness or covetousness, let it not even be named among you, as is fitting for saints; neither filthiness, nor foolish talking, nor coarse jesting, which are not fitting, but rather giving of thanks. For this you know, that no fornicator, unclean person, nor covetous man, who is an idolater, has any inheritance in the kingdom of Christ and God." (Ephesians 5:2–5)

James

James gives us a similar warning:

> *"Therefore submit to God. Resist the devil and he will flee from you. Draw near to God and He will draw near to you. Cleanse your hands, you sinners; and purify your hearts, you double-minded."*
> (James 4:7–8)

Peter

Peter equally emphasizes the need for holiness:

> *"but as He who called you is holy, you also be holy in all your conduct, because it is written, 'Be holy, for I am holy.' And if you call on the Father, who without partiality judges according to each one's work, conduct yourselves throughout the time of your stay here in fear; knowing that you were not redeemed with corruptible things, like silver or gold, from your aimless conduct received by tradition from your fathers, but with the precious blood of Christ, as of a lamb without blemish and without spot. He indeed was foreordained before the foundation of the world, but was manifest in these last times for you . . . "*
> (1 Peter 1:15–20)

John

In order to abide in Jesus and His love, John tells us we must keep His commandments:

> *"If you keep My commandments, you will abide in My love, just as I have kept My Father's commandments and abide in His love. These things I have spoken to you, that My joy may remain in you, and that your joy may be full. This is My commandment, that you love one another as I have loved you. Greater love has no one than this, than to lay down one's life for his friends. You are My friends if you do whatever I command you."*
> (John 15:10–14)

Judgment by fruit

If we abide in Jesus, we bear much fruit, but if we do not abide in Him, we are like a branch that is cut down and then withers:

> *"I am the vine, you are the branches. He who abides in Me, and I in him, bears much fruit; for without Me you can do nothing. If anyone does not abide in Me, he is cast out as a branch and is withered; and they gather them and throw them into the fire, and they are burned."*   (John 15:5–6)

The Apostle John, who was also known as the Apostle of love, was very definite about the issue of holiness:

> *"In this the children of God and the children of the devil are manifest: Whoever does not practice righteousness is not of God, nor is he who does not love his brother."*   (1 John 3:10)

If we keep the commandments of God, we abide in Him:

> *"Now he who keeps His commandments abides in Him, and He in him. And by this we know that He abides in us, by the Spirit whom He has given us."*   (1 John 3:24)

Disobedient Christians

Paul gives us a warning concerning those who claim to be Christians but fail to do the will of God, the Father:

> *"Moreover, brethren, I do not want you to be unaware that all our fathers were under the cloud, all passed through the sea, all were baptized into Moses in the cloud and in the sea, all ate the same spiritual food, and all drank the same spiritual drink. For they drank of that spiritual Rock that followed them, and that Rock was Christ. But with most of them God was not well pleased, for their bodies were scattered in the wilderness. Now these things became our examples, to the intent that we should not lust after evil things as they also lusted. And do not become idolaters as were some of them. As it is written, 'The people sat down to eat and drink, and rose up to play.' Nor let us commit sexual immorality, as some of them did, and in one day twenty-three thousand fell; nor let us tempt Christ, as some of them also tempted, and were destroyed by serpents; nor complain, as some of them also complained, and were destroyed by the destroyer. Now all these things happened to them as examples, and they were written for our admonition, upon whom the ends of the ages have come."*   (1 Corinthians 10:1–11)

Willful sin

That is why the writer to the Hebrews is so specific about willful sin:

> *"For if we sin willfully after we have received the knowledge of the truth, there no longer remains a sacrifice for sins, but a certain fearful expectation of judgment, and fiery indignation which will devour the adversaries. Anyone who has rejected Moses' law dies without mercy on the testimony of two or three witnesses. Of how much worse punishment, do you suppose, will he be thought worthy who has trampled the Son of God underfoot, counted the blood of the covenant by which he was sanctified a common thing, and insulted the Spirit of grace? For we know Him who said, 'Vengeance is Mine, I will repay,' says the Lord. And again, 'The Lord will judge His people.' It is a fearful thing to fall into the hands of the living God."*
>
> (Hebrews 10:26–31)

God has promised us in His word that we will never face any test that we cannot deal with:

> *"No temptation has overtaken you except such as is common to man; but God is faithful, who will not allow you to be tempted beyond what you are able, but with the temptation will also make the way of escape, that you may be able to bear it."*
>
> (1 Corinthians 10:13)

But, if we do fall, there is, as we have already seen in 1 John 1:9 quoted earlier in the chapter, the offer of complete forgiveness.

Obedience

From the above scriptures, it can be concluded that it is only those Christians who do the will of God who can expect to hear the words, *"Well done, good and faithful servant:"*

> *"Therefore whoever hears these sayings of Mine, and does them, I will liken him to a wise man who built his house on the rock: and the rain descended, the floods came, and the winds blew and beat on that house; and it did not fall, for it was founded on the rock. But everyone who hears these sayings of Mine, and does not do them, will be like a foolish man who built his house on the sand: and the rain descended, the floods came, and the winds blew and beat on that house; and it fell. And great was its*

fall. And so it was, when Jesus had ended these sayings, that the people were astonished at His teaching . . . "

(Matthew 7:24–28)

Thus, obedience to Jesus Christ is an essential part of our walk with Him. It is not sufficient to say simply that we believe in Jesus Christ in an intellectual way. To believe in Him means we must cling to Him, trust in Him and rely upon Him. As we do so, we will want to obey Him and His word. Then we need have no fear of any condemnation at the judgment seat of Christ.

Summary

1. We shall all stand before the judgment seat of Christ.

2. If judgment is to begin at the house of God, what will be the end of those who do not obey the gospel of God?

3. When we appear before the judgment seat of Christ, each one of us will be rewarded according to the things we have done while here on earth, whether good or bad.

4. The fear of God is the beginning of wisdom.

5. The fear of God is to hate evil.

6. One day all the secrets of our heart will be brought to the light.

7. Many who claim to be followers of Jesus Christ will be disowned by Him on the last day because they lived without any regard to God's laws.

8. We should be ready at all times to meet the Lord.

9. Jesus Christ is the vine.

10. Our conduct should in every way be pleasing to God. We should avoid deliberate sin.

11. We should bear fruit.

12. Disobedient Christians will be judged accordingly.

13. If we sin willfully after we have received a knowledge of the truth there no longer remains a sacrifice for sins.

14. Only those Christians who do the will of God can expect to hear the words, *"Well done, good and faithful servant."*

Chapter 26

The Judgment of Works

The book of remembrance

A reference to God's book of remembrance is made in Malachi, the last book of the Old Testament:

> "Then those who feared the LORD spoke to one another,
> And the LORD listened and heard them;
> So a book of remembrance was written before Him
> For those who fear the LORD and who meditate on His name."
> (Malachi 3:16)

Of those whose names are written in this book God says:

> "'They shall be Mine,' says the LORD of hosts,
> 'On the day that I make them My jewels.
> And I will spare them
> As a man spares his own son who serves him.'"
> (Malachi 3:17)

This is God's promise to those who obey Him.

God will make a distinction

We are then reminded of how God will make a distinction between those who serve Him and those who do not:

> "Then you shall again discern
> Between the righteous and the wicked,
> Between one who serves God
> And one who does not serve Him."
> (Malachi 3:18)

The judgment seat of Christ

Returning to the theme of judgment, as we have seen, Paul states clearly that each Christian will face God's judgment:

> *"For we must all appear before the judgment seat of Christ, that each one may receive the things done in the body, according to what he has done, whether good or bad. Knowing, therefore, the terror of the Lord, we persuade men; but we are well known to God, and I also trust are well known in your consciences."*
>
> (2 Corinthians 5:10–11)

When we turn to Jesus Christ, we should become a new creation in Him:

> *"Therefore, if anyone is in Christ, he is a new creation; old things have passed away; behold, all things have become new."*
>
> (2 Corinthians 5:17)

Many people glibly say they are a new creation in Jesus Christ without really recognizing the need to take up their cross daily and follow Him, to hate sin and do the will of God.

Although we are not saved by our works, once we have turned to Jesus Christ, then God certainly expects us to demonstrate the fruit of good works in our lives.

Jesus gives us clear teaching on works in two parables, namely the parable of the talents and the parable of the minas.

Parable of talents

In Matthew 25 Jesus describes three servants who were each given talents by their master:

> *"And to one he gave five talents, to another two, and to another one, to each according to his own ability; and immediately he went on a journey."* (Matthew 25:15)

A "talent' was a large sum of money in those days.

The one who received five talents went and traded them, making a further five, and the one who had received two talents also used them profitably, gaining two more. However, the servant who had received one talent dug a hole in the ground and hid his lord's money.

When the lord returned to settle accounts with his servants, he said to the one who had gained five more talents:

"Well done, good and faithful servant; you were faithful over a few things, I will make you ruler over many things. Enter into the joy of your lord."   (Matthew 25:21)

Similarly, he said to the one who had made a further two talents:

"Well done, good and faithful servant; you have been faithful over a few things, I will make you ruler over many things. Enter into the joy of your lord."   (Matthew 25:23)

The third servant tried to justify himself by making this excuse:

"Lord, I knew you to be a hard man, reaping where you have not sown, and gathering where you have not scattered seed. And I was afraid, and went and hid your talent in the ground. Look, there you have what is yours."   (Matthew 25:24–25)

The response of the lord was to call him a *"wicked and a lazy servant."* He told him that at least he should have deposited the money with the bankers so that he would have received interest. He commanded the talent to be taken from that servant and given to the one who had doubled his five to ten.

His final statement, however, is the one with which we must be most concerned:

"'And cast the unprofitable servant into the outer darkness. There will be weeping and gnashing of teeth.'"   (Matthew 25:30)

Parable of the minas

In this parable there are ten servants mentioned, although only three of them are finally discussed. Each of the ten servants received a mina (coin). When the nobleman returned, he called for the servants to find out how much each of them had gained by trading. The first said that his mina had earned ten minas. Here again, the response of his master was:

"Well done, good servant; because you were faithful in a very little, have authority over ten cities."   (Luke 19:17)

The second came forward saying, *"Master, your mina has earned five minas."* The master was pleased:

"Likewise he said to him, 'You also be over five cities.'"
(Luke 19:19)

However, the third one, who had kept the mina in a hand-kerchief, made this excuse:

> *"For I feared you, because you are an austere man. You collect what you did not deposit, and reap what you did not sow."*
>
> (Luke 19:21)

The response of the master was immediate:

> *"And he said to him, 'Out of your own mouth I will judge you, you wicked servant. You knew that I was an austere man, collecting what I did not deposit and reaping what I did not sow. Why then did you not put my money in the bank, that at my coming I might have collected it with interest?'"*
>
> (Luke 19:22–23)

The nobleman commanded those who stood by to take the mina from this last servant and give it to him who had ten.

Rewards

In the first parable, the faithful servants were told that they would be made rulers over many things. In the second parable, their reward was in exact proportion to what they had earned, namely, in the first case the servant was to have authority over ten cities, while the second servant was to have authority over five cities.

It is clear from these parables that God intends that those who are faithful to Him and carry out His works will be given positions of authority in Christ's coming kingdom.

The second parable does not specifically say what happened finally to the wicked servant but it is fair to assume that he too was thrown out of his master's presence.

After giving the parable of the talents, Jesus then went on to speak of His *"brethren."*

Sheep and goats

Speaking of the time when the nations (or peoples) will be gathered before Him, Jesus explains that He will separate them one from another as a shepherd divides the sheep from the goats. The sheep will be placed on His right hand but the goats on His left.

Those on the right hand will be told that they will inherit the kingdom prepared for them from the foundation of the world. The reason for this decision appears to be based on works:

"for I was hungry and you gave Me food; I was thirsty and you gave Me drink; I was a stranger and you took Me in; I was naked and you clothed Me; I was sick and you visited Me; I was in prison and you came to Me." (Matthew 25:35–36)

The righteous seem surprised by this. They ask:

" 'Lord, when did we see You hungry and feed You, or thirsty and give You drink? When did we see You a stranger and take You in, or naked and clothe You? Or when did we see You sick, or in prison, and come to You?' " (Matthew 25:37–39)

The response that Jesus gives is quite surprising:

"And the King will answer and say to them, 'Assuredly, I say to you, inasmuch as you did it to one of the least of these My brethren, you did it to Me.' " (Matthew 25:40)

The "brethren" of Jesus

Here, Jesus describes the hungry, the thirsty, the stranger, the naked, the sick and those in prison as His *"brethren."* It is used here in the same wider sense as the term "brothers" in the following verses:

"And it was told Him by some, who said, 'Your mother and Your brothers are standing outside, desiring to see You.' But He answered and said to them, 'My mother and My brothers are these who hear the word of God and do it.' " (Luke 8:20–21)

It equates with the wider use of the word "neighbor" in the parable of the good Samaritan as the one who showed mercy on the man who fell among thieves and was stripped of his clothing, wounded and left half dead. While the priest and Levite ignored the man, it was a Samaritan who had compassion on him. The story prompts the following dialogue between the lawyer who asked the original question and Jesus:

" 'So which of these three do you think was neighbor to him who fell among the thieves?' And he said, 'He who showed mercy on him.' Then Jesus said to him, 'Go and do likewise.' "
(Luke 10:36–37)

Thus, we find Jesus describing a particular group of people in one sense as His brethren. (Of course, this does not mean that these people are the sons and daughters of God. To be a son or daughter of God a person must be born again of the Spirit of God.)

Those who fail to take care of those in need are told:

> *"Depart from Me, you cursed, into the everlasting fire prepared for the devil and his angels ... "*   (Matthew 25:41)

On that day the people who are called the goats will ask Jesus when they failed to take care of Him and He will answer:

> *" 'Assuredly, I say to you, inasmuch as you did not do it to one of the least of these, you did not do it to Me.' And these will go away into everlasting punishment, but the righteous into eternal life."*   (Matthew 25:45–46)

This aspect of God's judgment is totally consistent with the rest of Scripture.

Results of concern for the poor

Praising God for the man who fears the Lord and delights greatly in His commandments, the psalmist points to one aspect of his obedience as his concern for the poor:

> *"Praise the LORD!*
> *Blessed is the man who fears the LORD,*
> *Who delights greatly in His commandments ...*
> *He has dispersed abroad,*
> *He has given to the poor ... "*   (Psalm 112:1, 9)

This concern has the following results:

> *"His righteousness endures forever;*
> *His horn will be exalted with honor."*   (Psalm 112:9)

> *"He who has pity on the poor lends to the LORD,*
> *And He will pay back what he has given."*   (Proverbs 19:17)

Paul quotes Psalm 112:9 in 2 Corinthians 9:9 in order to encourage a similar generosity in the church there.

God's fast

In Isaiah 58 the prophet Isaiah turns to the subject of fasting.

The people of Israel were not fasting in the way God intended and He is angry with them:

> *"Indeed you fast for strife and debate,*
> *And to strike with the fist of wickedness.*
> *You will not fast as you do this day,*
> *To make your voice heard on high."*   (Isaiah 58:4)

This was a false fast. God then describes the fast He has chosen:

> *"Is this not the fast that I have chosen:*
> *To loose the bonds of wickedness,*
> *To undo the heavy burdens,*
> *To let the oppressed go free,*
> *And that you break every yoke?*
> *Is it not to share your bread with the hungry,*
> *And that you bring to your house the poor who are cast out;*
> *When you see the naked, that you cover him,*
> *And not hide yourself from your own flesh?"*   (Isaiah 58:6–7)

Results of correct fasting

Those who fast in accordance with God's will, will experience the fulfillment of these wonderful promises:

> *"Then your light shall break forth like the morning,*
> *Your healing shall spring forth speedily,*
> *And your righteousness shall go before you;*
> *The glory of the* Lord *shall be your rear guard.*
> *Then you shall call, and the* Lord *will answer;*
> *You shall cry, and He will say, 'Here I am.'*
> *If you take away the yoke from your midst,*
> *The pointing of the finger, and speaking wickedness ..."*
>   (Isaiah 58:8–9)

Isaiah expands on this further:

> *"If you extend your soul to the hungry*
> *And satisfy the afflicted soul,*
> *Then your light shall dawn in the darkness,*
> *And your darkness shall be as the noonday."*   (Isaiah 58:10)

Once again the promise of God follows:

> *"The* Lord *will guide you continually,*
> *And satisfy your soul in drought,*

And strengthen your bones;
You shall be like a watered garden,
And like a spring of water, whose waters do not fail."

(Isaiah 58:11)

The weak

The Apostle Paul was very concerned about the care of the weak:

"I have shown you in every way, by laboring like this, that you must support the weak. And remember the words of the Lord Jesus, that He said, 'It is more blessed to give than to receive.'"

(Acts 20:35)

Works befitting repentance

After his encounter with God on the Damascus road, Paul was concerned to do works befitting repentance:

"but declared first to those in Damascus and in Jerusalem, and throughout all the region of Judea, and then to the Gentiles, that they should repent, turn to God, and do works befitting repentance."

(Acts 26:20)

The poor

This concern continued through his ministry, as these verses from Romans illustrate:

"But now I am going to Jerusalem to minister to the saints. For it pleased those from Macedonia and Achaia to make a certain contribution for the poor among the saints who are in Jerusalem. It pleased them indeed, and they are their debtors. For if the Gentiles have been partakers of their spiritual things, their duty is also to minister to them in material things."

(Romans 15:25–27)

Even though the churches in Macedonia and Achaia were poor, nevertheless, they were concerned for their less fortunate brethren, as Paul explained in 2 Corinthians 8:2–4:

"that in a great trial of affliction the abundance of their joy and their deep poverty abounded in the riches of their liberality. For I

bear witness that according to their ability, yes, and beyond their ability, they were freely willing, imploring us with much urgency that we would receive the gift and the fellowship of the ministering to the saints."

Works

James insists that our faith in Jesus Christ must result in works of obedience. He warns us against partiality toward the rich person who comes into our church, giving him a seat of honor, while we ask a poor, badly dressed person to stand on the edge, or sit at our feet. Finally he poses the question:

"Listen, my beloved brethren: Has God not chosen the poor of this world to be rich in faith and heirs of the kingdom which He promised to those who love Him?"　　　　　　　(James 2:5)

We can conclude from our reading of Scripture that the group of six categories of people, namely the hungry, the sick, the thirsty, the stranger, the naked and those in prison, have a special position in the heart of God. Those who claim to be Christians must share God's concern for these people.

Obviously, the whole of Scripture must be considered together. Those who seek to walk in obedience to God and do His will must obviously take heed of these scriptures.

Other works

James describes pure and undefiled religion in the following way:

"Pure and undefiled religion before God and the Father is this: to visit orphans and widows in their trouble, and to keep oneself unspotted from the world."　　　　　　　(James 1:27)

Faith without works is dead

"But do you want to know, O foolish man, that faith without works is dead?"　　　　　　　(James 2:20)

The rich

Paul cautions the rich that they should be equally prolific in good works:

"Let them do good, that they be rich in good works, ready to give, willing to share ... "   (1 Timothy 6:18)

Be zealous

In fact we should all be zealous in our good works:

"who gave Himself for us, that He might redeem us from every lawless deed and purify for Himself His own special people, zealous for good works."   (Titus 2:14)

They should not be a flash in the pan, but a constant feature of our lives:

"This is a faithful saying, and these things I want you to affirm constantly, that those who have believed in God should be careful to maintain good works. These things are good and profitable to men."   (Titus 3:8)

The letter to the Hebrews urges us to encourage one another to do good:

"And let us consider one another in order to stir up love and good works."   (Hebrews 10:24)

Thus, throughout Scripture, we are exhorted to maintain good works before God.

This truth can also be summed up in another way, namely as obedience to the commandment to love our neighbor as ourselves. As Paul says in Romans 13:

"Owe no one anything except to love one another, for he who loves another has fulfilled the law. For the commandments, 'You shall not commit adultery,' 'You shall not murder,' 'You shall not steal,' 'You shall not bear false witness,' 'You shall not covet,' and if there is any other commandment, are all summed up in this saying, namely, 'You shall love your neighbor as yourself.' Love does no harm to a neighbor; therefore love is the fulfillment of the law."   (Romans 13:8–10)

If we really show the love of Jesus to those who are our neighbors, that is the people in the world, by demonstrating compassion and carrying out good works, then we will be fulfilling this great commandment.

Those whose works shall be burned up and yet they shall be saved

In his first letter to the Corinthians, Paul describes the process of judgment by which our works will be tested:

> *"For no other foundation can anyone lay than that which is laid, which is Jesus Christ. Now if anyone builds on this foundation with gold, silver, precious stones, wood, hay, straw, each one's work will become clear; for the Day will declare it, because it will be revealed by fire; and the fire will test each one's work, of what sort it is. If anyone's work which he has built on it endures, he will receive a reward. If anyone's work is burned, he will suffer loss; but he himself will be saved, yet so as through fire."*
>
> (1 Corinthians 3:11-15)

There are two types of works described here, namely those of gold, silver and precious stones, as opposed to those made of wood, hay and straw. Those of gold, silver and precious stones will stand the test of fire, but those of wood, hay and straw will not survive.

This particular scripture prompts us to consider the type of works in which we are involved. Do they glorify God? Will they promote the kingdom of God, or are they works which glorify ourselves to some extent? If their sole aim is for the glory of God, then they will survive this test of fire, but if they are partly for our own glory, then they will not. God will not share His glory with anyone.

When we look at this aspect of judgment and compare it with the parable of the talents and minas, we see a difference between the Christian who tries to do something, even though part of his or her motivation may be wrong, and the person who does nothing. In the two parables quoted, the wicked servants did absolutely nothing. The Christian described in 1 Corinthians 3, however, has, at least, tried to do something.

Thus, we conclude with the parable of the man who built his house upon the rock:

> *"Therefore whoever hears these sayings of Mine, and does them, I will liken him to a wise man who built his house on the rock: and the rain descended, the floods came, and the winds blew and beat on that house; and it did not fall, for it was founded on the rock. But everyone who hears these sayings of Mine, and does not do them, will be like a foolish man who built his house on*

> *the sand: and the rain descended, the floods came, and the winds blew and beat on that house; and it fell. And great was its fall."*   (Matthew 7:24–27)

As Jesus has said:

> *"Therefore by their fruits you will know them."*
>   (Matthew 7:20)

Each of us needs to look carefully at the fruits of our lives. Are they truly in accordance with the word of God? Are our thoughts, actions and works based upon total obedience and submission to God, or are they based on our own selfish desires and motivations?

If it is the former and not the latter, then we can expect to hear the words, *"Well done, good and faithful servant."*

The wheat and tares

In one of His parables, Jesus describes the kingdom of heaven as like a man who sowed good seed in his field, but while he slept, his enemy came and sowed tares among the wheat. Tares look like wheat, but produce useless seed instead of good grain.

Here, Jesus is talking about those who appear to be Christians, but their hearts and actions are not consistent with the word of God.

The story continues:

> *"So the servants of the owner came and said to him, 'Sir, did you not sow good seed in your field? How then does it have tares?' He said to them, 'An enemy has done this.' The servants said to him, 'Do you want us then to go and gather them up?' But he said, 'No, lest while you gather up the tares you also uproot the wheat with them.' "*   (Matthew 13:27–29)

Finally, at the time of harvest, the owner would say to the reapers:

> *"First gather together the tares and bind them in bundles to burn them, but gather the wheat into my barn."*   (Matthew 13:30)

Explanation of the parable

When the disciples of Jesus asked Him to explain this parable He explained it as follows:

> *"He answered and said to them: 'He who sows the good seed is the Son of Man. The field is the world, the good seeds are the sons of the kingdom, but the tares are the sons of the wicked one. The enemy who sowed them is the devil, the harvest is the end of the age, and the reapers are the angels. Therefore as the tares are gathered and burned in the fire, so it will be at the end of this age. The Son of Man will send out His angels, and they will gather out of His kingdom all things that offend, and those who practice lawlessness, and will cast them into the furnace of fire. There will be wailing and gnashing of teeth. Then the righteous will shine forth as the sun in the kingdom of their Father. He who has ears to hear, let him hear!'"* (Matthew 13:37–43)

False Christians

Many people, even prominent Christians, today deny the physical resurrection of Jesus Christ or want to change the word of God concerning certain sins: they are in danger of being included in the category of hypocrites.

These and others who pose as Christians and yet actively work against the word of God are described by Scripture as those who offend and who practice lawlessness.

While they will be excluded from the kingdom of God, the righteous will shine forth like the sun in the kingdom of their Father.

Jesus further amplified this aspect of His teaching in the following parable:

> *"Again, the kingdom of heaven is like a dragnet that was cast into the sea and gathered some of every kind, which, when it was full, they drew to shore; and they sat down and gathered the good into vessels, but threw the bad away. So it will be at the end of the age. The angels will come forth, separate the wicked from among the just, and cast them into the furnace of fire. There will be wailing and gnashing of teeth."* (Matthew 13:47–50)

The angels separate

As the gospel of Jesus Christ is proclaimed, many respond, but not all live lives which are consistent with the word of God. At the end of the age, the angels will separate out the wicked from among the just and cast them into the furnace of fire.

In Psalm 1 we find a similar reference:

> *"The ungodly are not so,*
> *But are like the chaff which the wind drives away.*
> *Therefore the ungodly shall not stand in the judgment,*
> *Nor sinners in the congregation of the righteous."*
>
> (Psalm 1:4–5)

The ungodly and sinners will not remain in the presence of God.

Summary

1. A book of remembrance has been written before God for those who fear the Lord and who meditate on His name.

2. We must all appear before the judgment seat of Christ.

3. The parable of the talents describes three servants given talents by their master. Two of them did something with the talents, while the other did nothing and was condemned.

4. In the parable of the minas, two of the servants earned extra minas whereas the third did nothing and was condemned.

5. When all the nations are gathered before Jesus at the end of time, He will separate the "sheep" from the "goats." Those who helped the "brethren" of Jesus, the hungry, the thirsty, the stranger, the naked, the sick and those in prison, will inherit the kingdom, while those who failed to do so will be judged accordingly.

6. God promises to bless those who share their bread with the hungry.

7. We must also be concerned for the weak and the poor.

8. Pure and undefiled religion before God and the Father is to visit the orphans and the widows in their trouble and keep oneself unspotted from the world.

9. Faith without works is dead.

10. The rich should do good works.

11. We should be careful to maintain good works.

12. We should love our neighbor, that is the stranger or alien, as ourselves.

13. Paul describes two types of works, namely those of gold, silver and precious stones, as opposed to those made of wood, hay and straw. Those of gold, silver and precious stones will stand the test of fire, but those of wood, hay and straw will not survive. However, whichever category our works are, if we have sought to be obedient to God then we will still be saved.

14. In the parable of the wheat and tares, God tells us that He will leave the tares in His kingdom until the end, but then the angels will gather them out. The "tares" are the false Christians, who offend and practice lawlessness. They will be cast into the furnace of fire.

Chapter 27

Judgment for the Jews

In this chapter we will look at biblical prophecy concerning God's dealings with His chosen people, Israel.

Paul tells us in Romans 11:

> "For I do not desire, brethren, that you should be ignorant of this mystery, lest you should be wise in your own opinion, that blindness in part has happened to Israel until the fullness of the Gentiles has come in."
> (Romans 11:25)

Then we find this comment in verse 32:

> "For God has committed them all to disobedience, that He might have mercy on all."
> (Romans 11:32)

God will judge Israel

Towards the end of time and during the great tribulation, God will again judge His people, Israel. He will use the Gentiles as an instrument of that judgment. First of all, however, He will restore His people to their land. This has been promised many times in Scripture, but one example is Jeremiah 30:3:

> "'For behold, the days are coming,' says the LORD, 'that I will bring back from captivity My people Israel and Judah,' says the LORD. 'And I will cause them to return to the land that I gave to their fathers, and they shall possess it.'"

Another example is given in Ezekiel 20:34–46, a passage which describes how God will plead with His people:

> "'I will bring you out from the peoples and gather you out of the countries where you are scattered, with a mighty hand, with an

outstretched arm, and with fury poured out. And I will bring you into the wilderness of the peoples, and there I will plead My case with you face to face. Just as I pleaded My case with your fathers in the wilderness of the land of Egypt, so I will plead My case with you,' says the LORD God."

Israel passes under the rod

At that time God will purge all rebels out of Israel:

> *"I will make you pass under the rod, and I will bring you into the bond of the covenant; I will purge the rebels from among you, and those who transgress against Me; I will bring them out of the country where they dwell, but they shall not enter the land of Israel. Then you will know that I am the LORD."*
>
> (Ezekiel 20:37–38)

The return of Israel is also prophesied in these further verses in Ezekiel:

> *"Then say to them, 'Thus says the LORD God: "Surely I will take the children of Israel from among the nations, wherever they have gone, and will gather them from every side and bring them into their own land; and I will make them one nation in the land, on the mountains of Israel; and one king shall be king over them all; they shall no longer be two nations, nor shall they ever be divided into two kingdoms again."'"*
>
> (Ezekiel 37:21–22)

Tribulation of Israel

Then Israel will begin to undergo great tribulation as God brings the Gentile nations against it:

> *"Therefore, son of man, prophesy and say to Gog, 'Thus says the LORD God: "On that day when My people Israel dwell safely, will you not know it? Then you will come from your place out of the far north, you and many peoples with you, all of them riding on horses, a great company and a mighty army. You will come up against My people Israel like a cloud, to cover the land. It will be in the latter days that I will bring you against My land, so that the nations may know Me, when I am hallowed in you, O Gog, before their eyes."'"*
>
> (Ezekiel 38:14–16)

The same prophecy is referred to in Zechariah 14:1–4:

> *"Behold, the day of the* LORD *is coming,*
> *And your spoil will be divided in your midst.*
> *For I will gather all the nations to battle against Jerusalem;*
> *The city shall be taken,*
> *The houses rifled,*
> *And the women ravished.*
> *Half of the city shall go into captivity,*
> *But the remnant of the people shall not be cut off from the city.*
> *Then the* LORD *will go forth*
> *And fight against those nations,*
> *As He fights in the day of battle.*
> *And in that day His feet will stand on the Mount of Olives,*
> *Which faces Jerusalem on the east.*
> *And the Mount of Olives shall be split in two,*
> *From east to west,*
> *Making a very large valley;*
> *Half of the mountain shall move toward the north*
> *and half of it toward the south."*

God intervenes

Ezekiel 37 promises that God will intervene:

> *"say to them, 'Thus says the* LORD *God: "Surely I will take the stick of Joseph, which is in the hand of Ephraim, and the tribes of Israel, his companions; and I will join them with it, with the stick of Judah, and make them one stick, and they will be one in My hand. And the sticks on which you write will be in your hand before their eyes.'" Then say to them, 'Thus says the* LORD *God: "Surely I will take the children of Israel from among the nations, wherever they have gone, and will gather them from every side and bring them into their own land; and I will make them one nation in the land, on the mountains of Israel; and one king shall be king over them all; they shall no longer be two nations, nor shall they ever be divided into two kingdoms again. They shall not defile themselves anymore with their idols, nor with their detestable things, nor with any of their transgressions; but I will deliver them from all their dwelling places in which they have sinned, and will cleanse them. Then they shall be My people, and I will be their God."'"*   (Ezekiel 37:19–23)

Return of Jesus

After these events have taken place, Jesus will return to the Mount of Olives, from which He ascended into heaven two thousand years ago.

Having intervened to protect them, God will plead with His people and then judge them:

> " 'As I live,' says the LORD God, 'surely with a mighty hand, with an outstretched arm, and with fury poured out, I will rule over you. I will bring you out from the peoples and gather you out of the countries where you are scattered, with a mighty hand, with an outstretched arm, and with fury poured out. And I will bring you into the wilderness of the peoples, and there I will plead My case with you face to face. Just as I pleaded My case with your fathers in the wilderness of the land of Egypt, so I will plead My case with you,' says the LORD God. 'I will make you pass under the rod, and I will bring you into the bond of the covenant; I will purge the rebels from among you, and those who transgress against Me; I will bring them out of the country where they dwell, but they shall not enter the land of Israel. Then you will know that I am the LORD.' "   (Ezekiel 20:33–38)

The rebels having been purged out, those left will recognize Jesus Christ as their Lord and Savior.

God destroys nations

The day on which God will destroy the nations that come against Jerusalem is vividly described in Zechariah 12:9–10:

> "It shall be in that day that I will seek to destroy all the nations that come against Jerusalem. And I will pour on the house of David and on the inhabitants of Jerusalem the Spirit of grace and supplication; then they will look on Me whom they pierced. Yes, they will mourn for Him as one mourns for his only son, and grieve for Him as one grieves for a firstborn."

Refining of Israel

The people of Israel will now look on Jesus whom their ancestors pierced. Having passed through the great tribulation, they will now be refined and will come into the eternal presence of God:

" 'And it shall come to pass in all the land,'
Says the LORD,
'That two-thirds in it shall be cut off and die,
But one third shall be left in it:
I will bring the one-third through the fire,
will refine them as silver is refined,
And test them as gold is tested.
They will call on My name,
And I will answer them.
I will say, "This is My people";
And each one will say, "The LORD is my God." ' "

(Zechariah 13:8–9)

That is why Paul is able to write:

"And so all Israel will be saved, as it is written:

'The Deliverer will come out of Zion,
And He will turn away ungodliness from Jacob;
For this is My covenant with them,
When I take away their sins.' "   (Romans 11:26–27)

Having thus been judged by God and reconciled to Him
through Jesus Christ, those of the Jews who turn to Jesus Christ
at this time will not need to undergo further judgment. This
wonderful reconciliation with God is foreseen by the prophet
Ezekiel:

"David My servant shall be king over them, and they shall all
have one shepherd; they shall also walk in My judgments and
observe My statutes, and do them. Then they shall dwell in the
land that I have given to Jacob My servant, where your fathers
dwelt; and they shall dwell there, they, their children, and their
children's children, forever; and My servant David shall be their
prince forever. Moreover I will make a covenant of peace with
them, and it shall be an everlasting covenant with them; I will
establish them and multiply them, and I will set My sanctuary in
their midst forevermore. My tabernacle also shall be with them;
indeed I will be their God, and they shall be My people. The
nations also will know that I, the LORD, sanctify Israel, when My
sanctuary is in their midst forevermore."   (Ezekiel 37:24–28)

Summary

1. God has caused partial blindness to come on Israel until Jesus returns.

2. Towards the end of time and during the great tribulation, God will judge His people Israel. He will use the Gentiles as an instrument of that judgment. Before this occurs, they will, however, have been restored to their own land.

3. God says that He will purge the rebels out of Israel.

4. The prophet, Ezekiel, prophesied the return of Israel to their land.

5. Then Israel will begin to undergo great tribulation as God brings the Gentile nations against it.

6. Jesus will intervene to fight on Israel's behalf against the nations which have come together to attack it. His feet will stand on the Mount of Olives which will be split in two, making a very large valley. Half the mountain will move towards the north and half towards the south.

7. Having intervened to protect the Jews, God will then plead with them before He judges them.

8. God will destroy those nations that come against Jerusalem.

9. God will refine the people of Israel. Two-thirds will be cut off and die, but one-third will be left. They will be refined as silver and tested as gold.

10. Then all Israel will be saved.

11. God promises to make peace with them and establish an everlasting covenant with them. He will multiply and establish the Jewish nation and set up His sanctuary in their midst forever.

Chapter 28

The Great White Throne Judgment

The second resurrection

We have seen that the righteous dead will participate in the first resurrection at the time of the second coming of Christ. The Bible then describes a second resurrection which will take place at the end of the one thousand years of Christ's millennial reign on earth. Those who did not participate in the first resurrection are not raised up until the end of the thousand years:

> *"But the rest of the dead did not live again until the thousand years were finished ..."* (Revelation 20:5)

During this time, Satan will have been bound in the bottomless pit. At the end of a thousand years he will be released from his prison and will go out to deceive the nations in the four corners of the earth. Throughout this period Jesus will have been ruling on the earth, but now Satan will stir up the last final rebellion. This rebellion will be crushed by Jesus and the devil will then be cast into the lake of fire and brimstone:

> *"They went up on the breadth of the earth and surrounded the camp of the saints and the beloved city. And fire came down from God out of heaven and devoured them. The devil, who deceived them, was cast into the lake of fire and brimstone where the beast and the false prophet are. And they will be tormented day and night forever and ever."* (Revelation 20:9–10)

Great white throne judgment

The great white throne judgment will now take place. It is described as follows:

> *"Then I saw a great white throne and Him who sat on it, from whose face the earth and the heaven fled away. And there was found no place for them. And I saw the dead, small and great, standing before God, and books were opened. And another book was opened, which is the Book of Life. And the dead were judged according to their works, by the things which were written in the books. The sea gave up the dead who were in it, and Death and Hades delivered up the dead who were in them. And they were judged, each one according to his works. Then Death and Hades were cast into the lake of fire. This is the second death. And anyone not found written in the Book of Life was cast into the lake of fire."* (Revelation 20:11–15)

The Greek word *Hades* is the same word as the Hebrew word *Sheol*. This is the place of temporary imprisonment for the departed spirits before their final resurrection and judgment.

It is clear from Revelation 6:8 that Death and Hades are persons:

> *"So I looked, and behold, a pale horse. And the name of him who sat on it was Death, and Hades followed with him. And power was given to them over a fourth of the earth, to kill with sword, with hunger, with death, and by the beasts of the earth."*

In the deliverance ministry we often find that the spirits of Death and Hades surround a person and, as we command the strong man named Death and Hades to leave, the individual is set free.

In this context Death can be described as a dark angel who comes to the unrighteous at their time of death and claims their spirit. Hades follows death and takes these spirits into the place of the same name.

At the end of the one thousand years, however, Death and Hades will deliver up the spirits of those whom they held captive.

Judgment

Two different groups of people will appear before the great white throne. First there will be those who did not rise with Christ at the time of His second coming. Death and Hades now deliver them up. Among them will be people such as Tyre and Sidon, for whom Jesus said it would be more tolerable on that day than for those of Chorazin and Bethsaida, who rejected Him:

> *"Then He began to rebuke the cities in which most of His mighty works had been done, because they did not repent: 'Woe to you, Chorazin! Woe to you, Bethsaida! For if the mighty works which were done in you had been done in Tyre and Sidon, they would have repented long ago in sackcloth and ashes. But I say to you, it will be more tolerable for Tyre and Sidon in the day of judgment than for you. And you, Capernaum, who are exalted to heaven, will be brought down to Hades; for if the mighty works which were done in you had been done in Sodom, it would have remained until this day. But I say to you that it shall be more tolerable for the land of Sodom in the day of judgment than for you.'"*   (Matthew 11:20–24)

Among them will be people like the Ninevites and the Queen of the South, who will rise up in the judgment and condemn those who did not repent at the preaching of Jesus:

> *"For as Jonah was three days and three nights in the belly of the great fish, so will the Son of Man be three days and three nights in the heart of the earth. The men of Nineveh will rise up in the judgment with this generation and condemn it, because they repented at the preaching of Jonah; and indeed a greater than Jonah is here."*   (Matthew 12:40–41)

The second group will be those who have lived and died on the earth during the one thousand years of the millennial reign. The fact that people will live and die during that period is clearly set out in Isaiah 65:

> *"No more shall an infant from there live but a few days,*
> *Nor an old man who has not fulfilled his days;*
> *For the child shall die one hundred years old,*
> *But the sinner being one hundred years old shall be accursed."*
>   (Isaiah 65:20)

No excuse

Those who have lived without God will have no excuse on that day when they appear before the great white throne. Paul tells us that every person knows about God in their heart of hearts:

> *"For since the creation of the world His invisible attributes are clearly seen, being understood by the things that are made, even His eternal power and Godhead, so that they are without excuse."* (Romans 1:20)

Those who do not hear the gospel

In the two thousand years since the death and resurrection of Jesus Christ there have been many who have never heard the gospel. It would seem that they will be judged according to whether they have walked in the light they have received:

> *"For there is no partiality with God. For as many as have sinned without law will also perish without law, and as many as have sinned in the law will be judged by the law (for not the hearers of the law are just in the sight of God, but the doers of the law will be justified; for when Gentiles, who do not have the law, by nature do the things in the law, these, although not having the law, are a law to themselves, who show the work of the law written in their hearts, their conscience also bearing witness, and between themselves their thoughts accusing or else excusing them) in the day when God will judge the secrets of men by Jesus Christ, according to my gospel."* (Romans 2:11–16)

Their name must be in the Book of Life

Anyone whose name is not found written in the Book of Life will be thrown into the lake of fire:

> *"And anyone not found written in the Book of Life was cast into the lake of fire."* (Revelation 20:15)

Lake of fire

After their resurrection and judgment, all the unrighteous dead are condemned to the lake of fire. The word for this is *Gehena*.

> *"But the cowardly, unbelieving, abominable, murderers, sexually immoral, sorcerers, idolaters, and all liars shall have their part in the lake which burns with fire and brimstone, which is the second death."* (Revelation 21:8)

This will include the unrighteous whom Jesus has gathered out of His kingdom:

> *"The Son of Man will send out His angels, and they will gather out of His kingdom all things that offend, and those who practice lawlessness, and will cast them into the furnace of fire. There will be wailing and gnashing of teeth."*   (Matthew 13:41–42)

Death and Hades cast into the lake of fire

Last of all Death and Hades are thrown into the lake of fire:

> *"Then Death and Hades were cast into the lake of fire. This is the second death."*   (Revelation 20:14)

Paul tells us in 1 Corinthians 26 that the last enemy to be destroyed will be Death. As the two angels, Death and Hades, are finally cast into the lake of fire, spiritual death will no longer exist.

Understanding God's judgment

It is clear that we cannot understand all aspects of God's judgment. Much of it is unknown to us, but from what has been revealed we can be certain that those who choose to follow Jesus Christ in true obedience and carry out His commands are assured of eternal life. As for the rest, it will be a matter for God's mercy and judgment. Just as when the Lord commanded Moses to make a sanctuary, which was a copy of the one in heaven, and that sanctuary included the mercy seat, so the judgment seat of God will also be a mercy seat.

God's mercy

The overriding principle of God's judgment is His mercy. When Moses went up Mount Sinai, and the Lord descended in the cloud and stood with him there, He gave him this revelation of Himself:

> *"And the Lord passed before him and proclaimed, 'The Lord, the Lord God, merciful and gracious, longsuffering, and abounding in goodness and truth, keeping mercy for thousands, forgiving iniquity and transgression and sin, by no means clearing the guilty, visiting the iniquity of the fathers upon the*

children and the children's children to the third and the fourth generation.'" (Exodus 34:6–7)

The psalmist has said:

"Oh, give thanks to the God of heaven!
For His mercy endures forever." (Psalm 136:26)

Undoubtedly God will grant mercy to those who deserve it. As Paul has said in Romans 11:33:

"Oh, the depth of the riches both of the wisdom and knowledge of God! How unsearchable are His judgments and His ways past finding out!"

The End

In 1 Corinthians 15 Paul makes this glorious summation of the end of the age:

"Now when all things are made subject to Him, then the Son Himself will also be subject to Him who put all things under Him, that God may be all in all." (1 Corinthians 15:28)

Thus, when all things have been made subject to Jesus Christ, He Himself will be subject to God, so that God may be all in all. This is set out in Ephesians 1:9–10:

"having made known to us the mystery of His will, according to His good pleasure which He purposed in Himself, that in the dispensation of the fullness of the times He might gather together in one all things in Christ, both which are in heaven and which are on earth – in Him

This shows us the perfect plan of God coming to final fruition. It has been God's master plan always to put everything under Christ and, in turn, for Christ to be subject to God Himself so that the perfect unity of the Godhead might be displayed.

Summary

1. After Christ has reigned for one thousand years on this earth, Satan will be released from his prison and will go out to deceive the nations in the four corners of the earth. He will stir up the final rebellion.

2. After this rebellion has been crushed by Jesus the devil will be cast into the lake of fire and brimstone.

3. Then there will be the great white throne judgment.

4. The remaining dead, small and great, will stand before God and the books will be opened.

5. Two different groups of people will appear before the great white throne. First there will be those who did not rise with Christ at the time of His second coming. They will be people such as those of Tyre and Sidon and also Chorazin, Bethsaida and Capernaum, as well as the men of Nineveh and the Queen of the South.

6. The second group of people will be those who have lived and died on the earth during the one thousand years of the millennial reign.

7. Those who have lived without God will have no excuse on that day when they appear before the great white throne.

8. Those who have not heard the gospel will be judged according to whether they have walked in the light which they have received.

9. Those whose names are not written in the Book of Life will be cast into the lake of fire.

10. Death and Hades will be cast into the lake of fire.

11. We do not understand all aspects of God's judgment but it is clear that those who follow Jesus Christ in true obedience and carry out His commands are assured of eternal life.

12. For everybody else, it is a matter of God's mercy and judgment.

13. At the very end of time, all things will be made subject to Jesus, then He Himself will be made subject to God who put all things under Him.

14. Everything in heaven and on earth will then be gathered together as one in Christ.

Index

Other Books by Bill Subritzky
Demons Defeated
Escape From Hell
I Believe in Miracles
The Secret of God's Anointing
Receiving the Gifts of the Holy Spirit
How to Receive the Baptism with the Holy Spirit
How to Know the Anointing of God
How to be Born Again
Ministering in the Power of the Holy Spirit
How to Overcome Fear
How to Cast out Demons and Break Curses
Miracle at Dubbo
How to Read the Bible in One Year
On the Cutting Edge – an autobiography

VHS Videos and Audio Cassettes
Are You Ready to Die? (58 min.)
Behold the Man (51 min.)
Escaping the Destroyer (54 min.)
How the Blood of Jesus Sets You Free (44 min.)
How to Enter God's Kingdom (55 min.)
How to Gain Immortality (51 min.)
How to Receive God's Invitation (52 min.)
How to Receive God's Love (56 min.)
Is Your Name in the Book of Life? (55 min.)
Out of the Darkness (39 min.)
Overcoming Torment (57 min.)
Rescue From the Storms of Life (36 min.)
The Secret of Being Accepted (54 min.)
Harvest Power Training Course
Crusade Miracles (25 min.)
The Bill Subritzky Story (55 min.)
How to be an Overcomer (48 min.)
Who is this Jesus? (55 min.)
Sons of the Kingdom (55 min.)
Fear or Faith? (55 min.)
The Fatal Choice (55 min.)
The Living God (55 min.)
Receiving God's Peace (45 min.)
Overcoming Fear (54 min.)
The Living Water (55 min.)
Finding the Doorway to God (49 min.)
Binding the Strong Men (55 min.)
What is Truth? (48 min.)

Thirsty People (45 min.)
Healed! (49 min.)
Healing Marriages and Family Relationships (90 min.)
Hindrances to Healing (90 min.)
Receiving the Gifts of the Holy Spirit (4 hours)
Deliverance from Demons (New Version) (5 hours)
Ministering in the Power of the Holy Spirit (5 hours)
(plus Seminar Manual)
Christian Women Today Seminar (3.5 hours)

For updated catalogue and price-list write to:

Dove Ministries
PO Box 48036
Blockhouse Bay
Auckland 1230
New Zealand
email: dove@doveministries.com

UK
New Wine Ministries
PO Box 17
Chichester
West Sussex PO20 6YB

USA
Grace Distributors Inc.
PO Box 39206
Denver
CO 80239-0206

If you have enjoyed this book and would like to help us
to send a copy of it and many other titles to needy
pastors in the **Third World**, please write for further
information or send your gift to:

Sovereign World Trust
PO Box 777, Tonbridge
Kent TN11 0ZS
United Kingdom

or to the **'Sovereign World'** distributor in your country.

Visit our website at **www.sovereign-world.org**
for a full range of Sovereign World books.